I0427485

Effective Trade Management Strategies

Table of Contents

Effective Trade Management Strategies

Many beginning traders devote a considerable amount of time to perfecting their trade entry signals. However, they often pay less attention to the crucial aspect of managing the trade once it is active. Open trade management is a key component of developing a successful trading system, as it plays a pivotal role in optimising a trader's performance. By focusing on open trade management, traders can more effectively balance the risks associated with each position, ensuring that profits are maximised while losses are minimised.

Effective trade management helps traders avoid common pitfalls, such as holding onto losing trades too long or exiting profitable trades too early. By implementing solid trade management strategies, traders can enhance their risk-reward ratios and increase the likelihood of achieving consistent trading success.

One crucial aspect of trade management is adapting to changing market conditions. Markets are dynamic and can shift rapidly, requiring traders to modify their strategies to maintain their edge. A flexible trade management approach allows traders to respond to these changes and maintain a consistently profitable trading system.

The Balance Between Profit Maximization and Risk Minimization

The primary goal of trade management is to strike a balance between profit maximisation and risk minimization. Traders must find a way to maximise the potential gains from their trades while minimising potential losses.

There is often a trade-off between these two objectives. For example, a trader may use a tight stop loss to minimise the risk of a large loss, but this can also increase the likelihood of being stopped out of a trade.

Why is Trade Management Important?

Risk Control: One of the primary functions of trade management is to control risk. By managing trades effectively, traders can ensure that losses do not spiral out of control and that the risk on each trade is kept within acceptable limits. This involves setting appropriate stop-loss orders, adjusting them as the market moves, and knowing when to cut losses.

Profit Maximisation: Trade management is not just about preventing losses; it's also about maximising gains. By effectively managing trades, traders can let their profits run and capture larger market moves. This might involve using trailing stops or scaling out of positions to lock in profits while still allowing a portion of the position the chance to capture further gains.

Psychological Benefits: Effective trade management helps in reducing emotional stress and decision-making errors. By having clear rules and strategies for managing trades, traders can avoid impulsive decisions driven by fear or greed. This leads to a more disciplined, systematic approach to trading, which is crucial for long-term success.

Adaptability: The financial markets are constantly changing, and trade management allows traders to adapt their strategies to varying market conditions. By adjusting stop-loss levels, profit targets, and other trade parameters, traders can respond to new information or shifts in market sentiment, thus aligning their trading strategies with the current market environment.

The Role of Trade Management in Trading Strategies

Trade management should be viewed as an integral part of your trading strategy, not as an afterthought. A well-thought-out trade management strategy will include rules for:

- Initial stop-loss placement and how to move these stops to reduce risk or lock in profits.
- Profit targets and how to adjust them based on changing market conditions.
- The use of trailing stops to secure profits while giving the trade room to grow.
- Conditions under which to exit a trade early, such as significant market news or unexpected events.

Trade management is a critical skill that all traders must develop to ensure long-term success in the markets. It allows traders to control risk, maximise profits, maintain discipline, and adapt to changing market conditions. By incorporating effective trade management strategies into your trading plan, you can improve your chances of becoming a profitable and consistent trader.

Aligning Trade Management with Trading Goals

Aligning trade management with your trading goals is fundamental to achieving long-term success in the markets. Your goals as a trader might range from seeking regular income, preserving capital, to achieving high growth. Each objective requires a tailored approach to trade management, reflecting the unique risk tolerance, time horizon, and profitability targets of each trader.

Defining Your Trading Goals

Before delving into the specifics of trade management, it's crucial to clearly define your trading goals. Are you trading for immediate income, or are you more focused on long-term capital appreciation? How much risk are you willing to take on for potential rewards? Your answers to these questions will shape your approach to each trade and the overall management strategy.

Income Trading Goals: If your goal is to generate regular income, your trade management strategy might focus on shorter-term trades, frequent profits, and tighter stop-loss orders to protect each trade's earnings.

Capital Preservation Goals: For traders aiming primarily at capital preservation, trade management strategies might lean more towards conservative position sizing, broader stop-loss parameters to withstand market volatility, and avoiding high-risk trades that could jeopardise the principal amount.

Growth Trading Goals: If your objective is capital growth, you might adopt a more aggressive trade management approach, allowing for wider stop-loss margins to give trades more room to grow and employing strategies like pyramiding to maximise profitable positions.

Integrating Trade Management Strategies with Goals

Once your trading goals are defined, integrate them with your trade management strategies:

Risk Management Alignment: Your trade management strategies should reflect your risk tolerance. For instance, if your risk tolerance is low, use trade management techniques such as tighter stop losses or smaller position sizes. Conversely, if you have a higher risk tolerance and are seeking substantial growth, you might allow for larger drawdowns and employ techniques like trailing stops to capture significant market moves.

Profit Target Alignment: Set your profit targets based on your trading goals. Income-focused traders may set smaller, more frequent profit targets, while growth-oriented traders might aim for larger gains and therefore set wider profit targets.

Time Horizon Alignment: Your trade management should also align with your time horizon. Short-term traders might use daily or hourly charts to manage trades, while long-term traders might base their trade management decisions on weekly or monthly charts.

Adaptation to Market Conditions: Your approach to trade management should be flexible enough to adapt to changing market conditions while still aligning with your overall trading goals. This involves being prepared to adjust your strategies in response to new information or market movements without losing sight of your long-term objectives.

Aligning your trade management strategies with your trading goals is not a one-time task but a continuous process of adaptation and refinement.

Overview of Different Trade Management Strategies

There are numerous trade management strategies that traders can employ to manage their positions and achieve their desired balance between profit maximisation and risk minimization. Some of the most common trade management strategies include:

Stop loss orders: Stop loss orders are pre-determined exit points set by traders to limit their losses if the market moves against them.

Trailing stops: A trailing stop is a type of stop loss order that moves with the market, allowing traders to lock in profits as the market moves in their favour.

Profit targets: Traders can set predetermined profit targets to exit their positions when the market reaches a certain level, ensuring they capture gains before the market potentially reverses.

Pyramiding: Pyramiding is a strategy where traders add to their positions as the market moves in their favour, increasing their exposure and potential profits.

Time-based exits: Time-based exits involve closing trades after a predetermined amount of time has elapsed, regardless of the current profit or loss.

Scaling in and out of positions: Scaling involves gradually entering or exiting trades, which can help manage risk and improve the overall risk-reward ratio.

Volatility-based exits: Traders can use measures of volatility, such as Average True Range or standard deviation, to adjust their exits according to market conditions.

Fundamental analysis exits: This strategy involves using fundamental analysis, such as earnings reports or economic data, to determine when to exit a trade.

Throughout this book, we will delve deeper into these trade management strategies, providing real-life case studies to illustrate their practical applications in various market conditions. By understanding and implementing these strategies, traders can develop a comprehensive approach to managing their trades and achieving consistent trading success.

Chapter Developing Your Trade Management System

Create a System that Suits your Personality

Trading is a delicate balance of advantages and compromises.

For instance, if you cash in when a stock is strong, you risk missing out on a substantial upswing. Conversely, holding onto it might mean watching those gains evaporate. Use the day's low as a benchmark, and you might end up selling just before the stock rebounds.

Aiming for consistent 20% profits ensures you never hit that elusive 100% return. And if you're eyeing those standout triple-digit gains, be ready for sizable setbacks and witnessing promising profits vanish.

Broad stops call for smaller investments.

Act prematurely, and your move might stall before it breaks out.

High volatility stocks promise lucrative returns but come with reduced size and heightened unpredictability.

Wait for the perfect moment, and the price might surge away from your entry.

A large investment means quicker depletion of resources and narrowed choices, while diversifying too much can leave you juggling numerous modest stakes.

Every choice brings its own opportunity costs and consequences.

Yet, trading isn't a binary game of "this or that". Consider diversifying strategies: cash in on some profits while letting others mature; make an initial investment and expand on a promising breakout; strategically position stops to minimise losses.

Dabble in both high and moderate volatility stocks for a balanced portfolio. It's crucial to align your strategies with your psychological strengths and constraints. Recognize what makes you deviate from your plan.

If consecutive losses shatter your confidence and consistency isn't your strong suit, why use a stringent stop? Such an approach could be a recipe for disappointment.

A vast majority lack the mental resilience to face repeated setbacks without faltering. A broader, more conservative approach might suit better, leading to a higher success rate, fewer losses, and enhanced clarity of thought.

Introduction to Position Sizing

Position sizing is a critical aspect of trade management and risk control. It determines the amount of capital invested in a single trade relative to the total trading capital. Effective position sizing is crucial because it helps manage the risk associated with a trade, ensuring that losses do not significantly impact the overall trading account. The primary goal of position sizing is to maximise profits while minimising the risk of ruin.

Understanding the Importance of Position Sizing

Risk Limitation: Proper position sizing ensures that the risk taken on each trade is proportionate to the trader's risk tolerance and account size. This means that a trader can survive a series of losses without depleting their trading capital significantly.

Performance Consistency: By using a consistent position sizing strategy, traders can achieve more stable returns. Large, erratic position sizes can lead to significant fluctuations in account balance, making it harder to recover from drawdowns.

Psychological Stability: Correct position sizing reduces emotional stress, as traders are less likely to experience significant losses that can lead to panic, fear, or greed-driven decisions.

Strategies for Effective Position Sizing

Percentage Risk Model: This model involves risking a certain percentage of the total trading capital on each trade. For example, if a trader decides to risk 2% of their capital and has a $50,000 account, they would risk $1,000 on each trade.

Volatility Adjustment: Adjust position size based on the volatility of the asset being traded. In more volatile markets, traders should reduce their position size to accommodate larger price swings, thus keeping the dollar risk consistent.

Dollar Amount Risk Model: Some traders prefer to risk a fixed dollar amount on each trade. This method is straightforward but does not adjust for the changing size of the trading account or the volatility of the market.

Equity Percentage Model: This method involves risking a percentage of the current trading account equity, allowing the risk level to grow or shrink dynamically with the account size.

Implementing Position Sizing in Your Trade Management System

Determine Your Risk Tolerance: Before setting your position size, understand your risk tolerance. This is typically a percentage of your total trading capital that you are willing to lose on a single trade.

Calculate Stop-Loss Placement: Determine where your stop-loss will be set for each trade based on technical or fundamental analysis. This will help define the risk in terms of the trade setup.

Use Position Sizing Formula: Utilize the chosen position sizing strategy to calculate the exact size of each trade. For the percentage risk model, for example, divide the dollar amount risked by the stop-loss distance.

Review and Adjust: Regularly review your position sizing strategy as your trading capital changes. Adjust your position sizes accordingly to ensure that they remain aligned with your risk tolerance and trading objectives.

Record Keeping: Maintain accurate records of your trades, including position sizes and outcomes. This data will be invaluable for evaluating the effectiveness of your position sizing strategy and making adjustments as needed.

Advantages and Disadvantages of Different Position Sizing Methods

Advantages:

- Helps manage risk by limiting the impact of individual trade losses.
- Allows for better risk-reward ratios by aligning trade size with potential gains and losses.
- Maintains discipline by preventing overtrading or undertrading.

Disadvantages:

- Requires accurate market analysis to determine optimal position size.
- Can be complex to implement, particularly for advanced methods like the Kelly Criterion.
- May not be suitable for all types of trading strategies or market conditions.

Best Practices for Implementing Position Sizing in Different Market Conditions

- Choose a position sizing method that aligns with your risk tolerance, trading strategy, and objectives.

- Regularly review and adjust your position sizing strategy based on changes in your account balance, trading strategy, or market conditions.

- Combine position sizing with other risk management techniques, such as stop loss orders or profit targets, to optimise trade outcomes.

- Be flexible and adapt your position sizing strategy to different market conditions. For example, consider reducing position size during periods of high volatility or when trading less liquid assets.

By implementing proper position sizing in their trading system, traders can effectively manage risk, maintain discipline, and improve the overall performance of their trading system.

The Essence of Adaptive Trade Management

Adaptive trade management is about flexibility and responsiveness. It's the ability to adjust your trading strategies based on the evolving market conditions. Markets are dynamic entities characterised by constant changes in volatility, trend directions, and liquidity levels. As such, a one-size-fits-all approach to trade management is often inadequate. Adaptive trade management, therefore, involves modifying your trade execution, risk levels, and exit strategies in real-time, ensuring they remain aligned with current market dynamics.

Key Components of Adaptive Trade Management

Assessing Market Volatility: Understanding and adapting to the level of market volatility is crucial. In high volatility conditions, wider stop losses may be necessary to avoid being prematurely stopped out due to market noise. Conversely, in lower volatility settings, tighter stops can be employed to protect profits and reduce risk.

Trend Assessment: The strength and direction of market trends can significantly impact your trade management decisions. In strong trending markets, employing trailing stops can allow you to capture more significant portions of the move. In range-bound markets, it might be more effective to employ fixed profit targets and tighter stops.

Liquidity Considerations: Market liquidity affects how you enter and exit trades. In highly liquid markets, large orders can be executed with minimal impact on the price. In less liquid markets, trade management strategies need to account for the increased cost of trading and the potential difficulty in entering or exiting positions.

Strategies for Adaptive Trade Management

Dynamic Stop-Loss and Profit Target Adjustments: Adjust your stop-loss orders and profit targets based on changing market conditions. This might mean widening your stop-loss during high volatility periods or tightening it when the market calms down.

Trailing Stops: Use trailing stops to lock in profits while allowing your position the room to grow. The key here is to set the trailing stop at a level that balances between capturing gains and giving the trade enough space to fluctuate.

Scaling In and Out: Adjust your market exposure based on current market analysis and predictions. This could involve scaling into a position as it moves in your favor or scaling out to take profits while letting the remainder of your position run.

Time-based Exits: Incorporate time elements into your trade management. For example, if a trade hasn't reached your profit target or stop-loss level within a predetermined period, you might exit the trade to avoid the risks of unexpected market moves.

Implementing Adaptive Trade Management

Continuous Market Analysis: Stay updated with market trends, news, and analyses. The more informed you are, the better you can adapt your trade management strategies to current market conditions.

Feedback Loops: Create a system where the outcomes of your trades feed back into your decision-making process. Analyse the effectiveness of your adaptive strategies and make necessary adjustments.

Risk Management: Always prioritise risk management, even when adapting to new market conditions. Ensure that changes in trade management strategies do not expose you to undue risk.

Technology Utilisation: Utilise trading tools and platforms that allow for automatic adjustments of stop losses, profit targets, and other trade management parameters based on predefined rules.

Modifying Trade Management Strategies Based on Changing Market Conditions and Personal Performance

- Market conditions: Assessing market trends, volatility, and liquidity to determine the most appropriate trade management techniques.

- Personal performance: Reviewing and analysing trading performance metrics, such as win rate, risk-reward ratio, and drawdown, to identify areas of improvement and implement necessary adjustments to trade management strategies.

The Role of Adaptive Trade Management in Risk Management

- **Flexibility:** Adaptive trade management allows traders to adapt their strategies to different market conditions, enhancing their ability to manage risk effectively.

- **Continuous improvement:** Regularly reviewing and adjusting trade management strategies based on personal performance helps traders identify and address weaknesses, ultimately improving risk management.

- **Mitigating losses:** Adaptive trade management enables traders to make necessary changes to their strategies to limit losses and protect profits in changing market conditions.

Advantages and Disadvantages of Using Adaptive Trade Management

Advantages:

- **Responsiveness:** Adaptive trade management enables traders to quickly respond to changing market conditions, which can help improve overall trading performance.

- **Customization:** Traders can tailor their trade management strategies to their individual trading styles and risk tolerance levels, increasing the likelihood of success.

- **Learning opportunity:** Adaptive trade management encourages traders to review and learn from their trading performance, ultimately leading to better risk management and decision-making.

Disadvantages:

- **Complexity:** Adaptive trade management can be complex, as it requires traders to continually assess market conditions and adjust their strategies accordingly.

- **Overfitting:** Traders may risk overfitting their strategies to specific market conditions, which may lead to poor performance when market conditions change.

- **Time-consuming:** Continuously analysing personal trading performance and modifying strategies can be time-consuming and may divert attention from other important trading tasks.

Best Practices for Implementing Adaptive Trade Management in Different Market Conditions

- **Regularly review trading performance:** Set aside time to analyse trading performance metrics and identify areas of improvement.

- **Develop a range of strategies:** Maintain a toolbox of trade management strategies that can be applied in different market conditions.

- **Stay informed:** Keep up-to-date with market news, economic events, and technical indicators to understand the current market environment and make informed adjustments to trade management strategies.

- **Be disciplined:** Implement changes to trade management strategies based on objective analysis rather than emotions or impulsive decisions.

- **Avoid overfitting:** Be cautious not to overly customise strategies to fit specific market conditions, as this may lead to poor performance when conditions change.

Chapter - Setting the Foundation

Stop Loss Orders

Definition and Explanation

A stop loss order is a protective order placed by traders to automatically close a trade if the market moves against them by a predetermined amount. The primary purpose of a stop loss order is to limit potential losses on a trade, thereby preserving capital and managing risk.

Types of Stop Loss Orders

There are several types of stop loss orders, including:

- **Fixed Stop Loss:** A fixed stop loss order is set at a specific price level, usually a predetermined distance from the entry price. This is the most straightforward and commonly used type of stop loss order.

- **Percentage Stop Loss:** A percentage stop loss order is set at a specified percentage away from the entry price. This approach adjusts the stop loss level based on the asset's price, helping to maintain a consistent risk across different trades.

- **Volatility-Based Stop Loss:** A volatility-based stop loss order takes market volatility into account when setting the stop loss level. Traders often use the Average True Range (ATR) indicator to measure volatility and set their stop loss at a multiple of the ATR value away from the entry price.

The Role of Stop Loss Orders in Risk Management

Stop loss orders play a crucial role in risk management by:

- **Limiting Losses:** Stop loss orders help traders limit their losses on individual trades, preventing any single trade from significantly impacting the overall account balance.

- **Providing Discipline:** Stop loss orders enforce discipline by automatically closing trades when the predetermined loss threshold is reached, preventing traders from holding on to losing positions out of hope or fear.

- **Enabling Risk Control:** By setting stop loss orders based on the trader's risk tolerance, traders can control the maximum amount they are willing to risk on each trade, ensuring that they stay within their overall risk management parameters.

Advantages and Disadvantages of Using Stop Loss Orders

Advantages:

- **Loss Limitation:** Stop loss orders protect traders from large losses on individual trades, preserving capital and managing risk.

- **Emotion Control:** Stop loss orders help traders overcome emotional biases by automatically closing losing trades at predetermined levels.

- **Consistency:** Stop loss orders ensure that traders consistently apply their risk management rules across all trades.

Disadvantages:

- **Premature Exits:** Stop loss orders may sometimes close trades too early if the market experiences temporary fluctuations, causing traders to miss potential gains.

- **Slippage:** In fast-moving or illiquid markets, stop loss orders may be executed at a worse price than anticipated, resulting in larger losses than expected.

- **No Guarantees:** In extreme market conditions, such as gaps or flash crashes, stop loss orders may not be executed at all, exposing traders to greater losses.

Best Practices for Implementing Stop Loss Orders in Different Market Conditions

- Choose the appropriate type of stop loss order based on your trading strategy, risk tolerance, and market conditions.

- Set stop loss levels based on technical analysis, such as support and resistance levels, moving averages, or other relevant indicators.

- Be prepared to adjust stop loss levels if market conditions change, but avoid constantly adjusting stop losses out of fear or greed.

- Consider using wider stop loss levels in volatile markets to avoid premature exits due to temporary fluctuations.

- Always use stop loss orders in conjunction with other risk management techniques, such as position sizing and profit targets, to create a comprehensive risk management strategy.

By using stop loss orders effectively, traders can limit their losses, maintain discipline, and enhance their overall risk management strategy.

Definition and Explanation

Trailing stops are a type of stop loss order that automatically adjusts as the market moves in favour of the trader's position. The primary purpose of a trailing stop is to lock in profits while still allowing the trade room to run, potentially increasing gains. As the market moves in the trader's favour, the trailing stop follows at a predetermined distance, effectively "trailing" the market price. If the market reverses and hits the trailing stop, the trade is closed, and the profits are secured.

Types of Trailing Stops

There are several types of trailing stops that traders can use, depending on their preferences and trading strategies:

- **Fixed Trailing Stops:** A fixed trailing stop maintains a constant distance (in points or pips) from the market price. As the market moves in the trader's favour, the stop loss is adjusted by the same number of points or pips.

- **Percentage Trailing Stops:** A percentage trailing stop adjusts the stop loss based on a percentage of the market price or the trader's entry price. This type of trailing stop can be useful when trading assets with varying price ranges or volatility.

- **Volatility-Based Trailing Stops:** Volatility-based trailing stops use a measure of market volatility, such as Average True Range (ATR) or standard deviation, to determine the distance of the trailing stop from the market price. As market volatility increases, the trailing stop will adjust further away from the market price to allow the trade more room to breathe.

The Role of Trailing Stops in Risk Management

Trailing stops play a crucial role in risk management by enabling traders to protect their profits while maintaining exposure to potentially larger gains. By automatically adjusting the stop loss as the market moves in the trader's favour, trailing stops help to minimise the risk of giving back profits if the market reverses.

Additionally, trailing stops can help traders manage their emotions by removing the need for manual intervention in adjusting stop loss levels. This can prevent traders from holding onto losing trades too long or exiting winning trades too soon due to fear or greed.

Advantages and Disadvantages of Using Trailing Stops

Advantages:

- Protects profits by automatically locking in gains as the market moves in the trader's favour.
- Allows for potentially larger gains by giving winning trades room to run.
- Reduces emotional decision-making by automatically adjusting stop loss levels.
- Can be customised to suit different trading strategies and risk tolerances.

Disadvantages:

- May result in premature trade exits if the trailing stop is set too close to the market price.
- Can be vulnerable to market noise and short-term fluctuations, potentially triggering unnecessary stop loss orders.
- May not be suitable for all types of trading strategies or market conditions.

Best Practices for Implementing Trailing Stops in Different Market Conditions

- Choose the appropriate type of trailing stop based on your trading strategy, asset, and market conditions. For instance, volatility-based trailing stops may be more effective in highly volatile markets, while fixed or percentage trailing stops might be suitable for less volatile assets.

- Set the trailing stop distance according to your risk tolerance and the characteristics of the asset you're trading. The trailing stop should be far enough from the market price to avoid being triggered by normal market fluctuations but close enough to protect profits.

- Test and optimise your trailing stop settings using historical data and backtesting to find the most effective parameters for your trading strategy.

- Combine trailing stops with other risk management techniques, such as position sizing and diversification, to create a comprehensive risk management plan.

- Continuously monitor and review your trailing stop strategy's performance, making adjustments as needed to improve its effectiveness in different market conditions

Profit Targets

Profit targets are pre-determined price levels at which traders plan to exit a trade to realise gains. These targets are typically based on technical or fundamental analysis and are set before entering a trade. Profit targets help traders define their trading objectives, manage risk, and maintain discipline by providing a clear exit point for successful trades.

Setting Realistic Profit Targets Based on Market Analysis

To set realistic profit targets, traders should consider the following factors based on market analysis:

- **Technical Analysis:** Traders can use technical indicators, chart patterns, and support and resistance levels to identify potential profit targets. For example, a trader might set a profit target at a significant resistance level for a long trade or a support level for a short trade.

- **Fundamental Analysis:** Traders can use fundamental analysis to determine the fair value of an asset or identify potential market catalysts that could impact the asset's price. This information can help traders set profit targets based on the expected impact of news events or changes in market conditions.

- **Risk-Reward Ratio:** Traders should consider the risk-reward ratio when setting profit targets. A favourable risk-reward ratio ensures that the potential gains outweigh the potential losses in a trade. For instance, if a trader risks 50 pips to make 100 pips, the risk-reward ratio is 2:1.

- **Volatility:** Traders should account for market volatility when setting profit targets. In more volatile markets, profit targets might need to be set further away from the entry price to accommodate larger price swings.

The Role of Profit Targets in Risk Management

Profit targets play a crucial role in risk management by helping traders:

- Define Trading Objectives: By setting profit targets, traders establish clear goals for each trade, helping them maintain discipline and focus.

- Manage Risk-Reward Ratio: Profit targets help traders achieve a favourable risk-reward ratio by ensuring that potential gains are proportionate to the risk taken in a trade.

- Avoid Emotional Decision-Making: With predetermined profit targets, traders can reduce the likelihood of making impulsive decisions driven by fear or greed.

Advantages and Disadvantages of Using Profit Targets

Advantages:

- Provides clear exit points for successful trades.
- Helps maintain discipline and focus by establishing trading objectives.
- Ensures a favourable risk-reward ratio.
- Reduces emotional decision-making in trade management.

Disadvantages:

- May limit potential gains by forcing traders to exit trades before the market reaches its full potential.
- Requires accurate market analysis to set realistic profit targets.
- May not be suitable for all types of trading strategies or market conditions.

Best Practices for Implementing Profit Targets in Different Market Conditions

Use a combination of technical and fundamental analysis to set realistic profit targets that align with market conditions and the asset's potential.

Consider market volatility when setting profit targets, allowing for larger price swings in more volatile markets.

Maintain a favourable risk-reward ratio by ensuring that potential gains outweigh potential losses in each trade.

Regularly review and adjust profit targets based on changes in market conditions, asset performance, or trading strategy.

Combine profit targets with other trade management strategies, such as stop loss orders or trailing stops, to manage risk effectively and optimise trade outcomes.

By incorporating profit targets into their trade management strategies, traders can better manage risk, maintain discipline, and improve the overall performance of their trading system.

Break-Even Stops

Break-even stops are a trade management technique that automatically closes a trade when it reaches the price level at which the trade was entered. This strategy is designed to protect traders' profits and limit potential losses by ensuring that a trade is closed as soon as it reaches a break-even point.

Protecting Profits and Limiting Losses

Break-even stops can be set by traders at the point at which the trade was entered, and once the price reaches this level, the trade is automatically closed. This strategy helps to protect traders' profits and limit potential losses by ensuring that a trade is closed as soon as it reaches a break-even point.

The Role of Break-Even Stops in Risk Management

Break-even stops play a crucial role in risk management by:

Protecting Profits

- By closing a trade at the break-even point, traders can ensure that they at least break even on the trade, regardless of future market movements.
- Limiting Losses
- If the market moves against the trader, break-even stops can help to limit potential losses by automatically closing the trade at the break-even point.

Balancing Risk and Reward

- This strategy enables traders to find a balance between protecting their profits and maintaining the potential for further gains.

Advantages of Using Break-Even Stops

Profit Protection
- Break-even stops allow traders to protect their profits and ensure that they at least break even on the trade, regardless of future market movements.

Ease of Use
- This strategy is easy to implement, as traders only need to set the break-even point once and the trade will be automatically closed if the price reaches this level.

Reduced Emotional Impact
- Break-even stops can help traders to remove the emotional impact of trading by automatically closing the trade when it reaches the break-even point.

Disadvantages of Using Break-Even Stops

Limited Profit Potential
- By automatically closing the trade at the break-even point, traders may miss out on larger gains if the market continues to move in their favour.

Lack of Flexibility
- Break-even stops offer limited flexibility in managing trades, as traders cannot adjust the point at which the trade is closed.

Over-reliance
- Traders may become too reliant on break-even stops, which can lead to poor decision-making and reduced effectiveness in managing risk.

Best Practices for Implementing Break-Even Stops in Different Market Conditions

- Define the break-even point at the price level at which the trade was entered.

- Combine break-even stops with other trade management strategies, such as partial profit taking or trailing stops, to create a comprehensive risk management plan.

- Monitor the performance of your break-even stop strategy and make adjustments as necessary to optimise trade outcomes and risk management.

- Stay disciplined and consistently apply your break-even stop strategy across all trades to ensure long-term success.

By incorporating break-even stops into your trade management toolkit, you can effectively protect your profits and limit potential losses. However, it is essential to recognize the limitations of break-even stops and use them in conjunction with other trading tools and risk management strategies to optimise your overall trading approach.

Partial Profit Taking

Definition and Explanation

Partial profit taking is a trade management technique where a trader closes a portion of a position to lock in profits while letting the remainder run. This strategy allows traders to capitalise on market movements, reduce risk exposure, and potentially benefit from further price moves in their favour.

Closing a Portion of a Position to Lock in Profits While Letting the Remainder Run

Traders can implement partial profit taking by setting predetermined profit levels or using technical indicators to signal when to close a portion of the position. Once the specified level is reached, a part of the trade is closed, securing profits, and the remaining position is allowed to run in the hope of additional gains.

The Role of Partial Profit Taking in Risk Management

Partial profit taking plays a crucial role in risk management by:

- **Locking in Profits:** By closing a portion of a position, traders can secure some profits and reduce the potential loss if the market reverses.

- **Reducing Exposure:** Partial profit taking reduces the trader's exposure to market risk by decreasing the size of the open position.

- **Balancing Risk and Reward:** This strategy enables traders to find a balance between securing profits and maintaining the potential for further gains.

Advantages and Disadvantages of Using Partial Profit Taking

Advantages

- **Profit Protection:** Partial profit taking allows traders to lock in some gains while still participating in potential market moves.
- **Flexibility:** This strategy offers flexibility in managing trades, as traders can adjust the portion of the position they close based on market conditions and their risk tolerance.
- **Reduced Risk Exposure:** By taking partial profits, traders can decrease their overall risk exposure, which can be beneficial during periods of increased market uncertainty.

Disadvantages

- **Lower Profit Potential:** By closing a portion of a position, traders may miss out on larger gains if the market continues to move in their favour.

- **Increased Complexity:** Managing partial profit taking can be more complex than using a single exit strategy, as traders need to monitor multiple profit levels and make decisions about when to close portions of their position.

- **Over-optimization:** Traders might be tempted to over-optimize their partial profit taking strategy, which can lead to poor decision-making and reduced effectiveness.

Best Practices for Implementing Partial Profit Taking in Different Market Conditions

- Define clear profit levels or technical indicators to signal when to take partial profits. These levels should be based on your analysis of the market and your risk tolerance.

- Determine the portion of the position you will close at each profit level. This decision should be based on your overall risk management strategy and trading goals.

- Monitor the performance of your partial profit taking strategy and make adjustments as necessary to optimise trade outcomes and risk management.

- Combine partial profit taking with other trade management strategies, such as stop loss orders or trailing stops, to create a comprehensive risk management plan.

- Stay disciplined and consistently apply your partial profit taking strategy across all trades to ensure long-term success.

By incorporating partial profit taking into your trade management toolkit, you can effectively manage risk, lock in profits, and potentially benefit from continued market moves. However, it is essential to recognize the limitations of partial profit taking and use it in conjunction with other trading tools and risk management strategies to optimise your overall trading approach.

Definition and Explanation

Risk-reward ratio analysis is a method used by traders to assess the potential reward of a trade compared to its associated risk. This ratio is calculated by dividing the potential profit (reward) by the potential loss (risk) and helps traders determine whether a trade is worth taking based on their risk tolerance and trading objectives.

Assessing the Potential Reward Compared to the Risk for Each Trade

To calculate the risk-reward ratio, traders must first determine the potential profit and potential loss for a given trade. The potential profit is the difference between the entry price and the target price, while the potential loss is the difference between the entry price and the stop-loss price. The risk-reward ratio is then calculated as follows:

Risk-Reward Ratio = Potential Profit / Potential Loss

A higher risk-reward ratio indicates a more favourable trade setup, as the potential reward is greater relative to the risk involved.

The Role of Risk-Reward Ratio Analysis in Trade Management

Risk-reward ratio analysis plays a crucial role in trade management by:

- **Helping traders assess the viability of a trade:** By comparing the potential reward to the associated risk, traders can determine whether a trade is worth taking based on their risk tolerance and objectives.

- **Aiding in setting stop-loss and profit target levels:** Risk-reward analysis can guide traders in setting appropriate stop-loss and profit target levels, ensuring that trades have a favourable risk-reward profile.

- **Supporting consistency and discipline:** Using risk-reward analysis can help traders maintain consistency in their trading approach, ensuring that they only take trades with a favourable risk-reward profile.

Advantages and Disadvantages of Using Risk-Reward Ratio Analysis

Advantages

- **Informed decision-making:** Risk-reward analysis provides traders with a quantitative method to assess the potential outcomes of a trade, allowing for more informed decision-making.

- **Improved risk management:** By focusing on trades with favourable risk-reward profiles, traders can improve their overall risk management and increase the likelihood of long-term success.

- **Enhanced discipline:** Using risk-reward analysis can help traders maintain discipline and avoid taking impulsive trades with unfavourable risk-reward profiles.

Disadvantages

- **Limited perspective:** Risk-reward analysis does not account for other factors that may impact trade outcomes, such as changing market conditions or the trader's ability to execute the trade effectively.

- **Overemphasis on individual trades:** Focusing too heavily on the risk-reward ratio for individual trades may cause traders to overlook the bigger picture and the overall performance of their trading system.

- **Incomplete analysis:** Risk-reward analysis alone may not provide a comprehensive assessment of trade viability, and traders should consider other factors, such as probability of success and market context.

Best Practices for Implementing Risk-Reward Ratio Analysis in Different Market Conditions

- Establish a minimum risk-reward ratio: Set a minimum acceptable risk-reward ratio based on your risk tolerance and trading objectives, and only take trades that meet or exceed this threshold.

- Consider the probability of success: In addition to the risk-reward ratio, consider the probability of a trade being successful, as this can provide a more comprehensive assessment of trade viability.

- Adjust risk-reward expectations based on market conditions: Be flexible in your risk-reward expectations, as different market conditions may require adjustments to your risk-reward criteria.

- Combine risk-reward analysis with other trade management tools: Use risk-reward analysis in conjunction with other trade management techniques and tools, such as stop-loss orders, position sizing, and trailing stops, to create a comprehensive risk management plan.

- Continuously evaluate and refine your risk-reward criteria: Periodically review your risk-reward criteria and adjust them as needed based on your trading performance, market conditions, and changes in your risk tolerance or trading objectives.

Chapter - Advanced Exit Strategies

Time-based Exits

Definition and Explanation

Time-based exits are a trade management strategy where traders exit their positions based on a predetermined time frame or event, rather than relying solely on price-based criteria such as stop loss orders or profit targets. This approach can help traders manage risk, maintain discipline, and avoid holding onto positions for too long.

Using Time-based Exits to Manage Trades

There are several ways to implement time-based exits in trading:

- **End-of-Day Exits:** Traders exit their positions at the end of the trading day, regardless of the trade's current profit or loss. This approach is commonly used in day trading, where traders aim to close all positions before the market close to avoid overnight risks.

- **Holding Period Limits:** Traders set a maximum holding period for their trades, exiting positions once the predetermined time frame has passed. This can help traders avoid holding onto losing positions for too long or staying in winning trades beyond their optimal exit point.

- **Time-based Profit Targets:** Traders set profit targets based on specific time intervals, such as hourly or daily price gains. This approach can help traders capture gains during specific market conditions, such as trending periods or high-volatility sessions.

The Role of Time-based Exits in Risk Management

Time-based exits can play a significant role in risk management by:

- **Reducing Exposure:** Time-based exits help traders limit their exposure to market risks, such as overnight gaps, news events, or sudden price movements.

- **Encouraging Discipline:** Time-based exits enforce a systematic approach to trade management, helping traders maintain discipline and avoid emotional decision-making.

- **Complementing Other Risk Management Strategies:** Time-based exits can be used in conjunction with other trade management strategies, such as stop loss orders and position sizing, to create a comprehensive risk management plan.

Advantages and Disadvantages of Using Time-based Exits

Advantages

- **Risk Reduction:** Time-based exits can help traders limit their exposure to market risks and reduce the impact of adverse price movements.

- **Discipline:** Time-based exits promote discipline by enforcing a systematic approach to trade management, preventing traders from holding onto positions based on emotions or hope.

- **Flexibility:** Time-based exits can be customised to suit various trading styles, timeframes, and market conditions, providing a versatile trade management tool.

Disadvantages

- **Premature Exits:** Time-based exits may sometimes close trades too early, causing traders to miss out on potential gains if the market continues to move in their favour.

- **Reduced Profit Potential:** By exiting trades based on time rather than price, traders may not capture the full profit potential of a trade.

- **Inefficiency:** In some cases, time-based exits may not be the most efficient way to manage trades, particularly when other risk management strategies, such as trailing stops or profit targets, might be more effective in specific market conditions.

Best Practices for Implementing Time-based Exits in Different Market Conditions

- Choose the appropriate time-based exit strategy based on your trading style, time frame, and market conditions.

- Combine time-based exits with other trade management strategies, such as stop loss orders and profit targets, to create a well-rounded risk management plan.

- Adjust your time-based exit criteria as needed to account for changing market conditions, but avoid making frequent changes based on emotions or recent trade outcomes.

- Monitor the performance of your time-based exit strategy and make adjustments as necessary to optimise trade outcomes and risk management.

- Stay disciplined and consistently apply your time-based exit strategy across all trades to ensure long-term success.

Volatility-based Exits

Definition and Explanation

Volatility-based exits are trade management techniques that use measures of market volatility to determine optimal exit points for open positions. By considering the level of price fluctuations, traders can adapt their exit strategies to account for changing market conditions, protecting profits, and minimising losses. Common volatility measures used for exit strategies include Average True Range (ATR) and standard deviation.

Using Volatility Measures to Adjust Exits

Average True Range (ATR): ATR is a measure of market volatility that calculates the average range between the high and low prices over a specified period. Traders can use the ATR to set trailing stops or to adjust their profit targets and stop-loss levels, depending on the current market volatility.

Standard Deviation: Standard deviation is a measure of price dispersion from the mean. By incorporating standard deviation into their exit strategies, traders can account for the changing levels of volatility in the market and adjust their stop-loss orders or profit targets accordingly.

The Role of Volatility-based Exits in Risk Management

Volatility-based exits play a significant role in risk management by:

- **Adapting to market conditions:** By considering market volatility, traders can adapt their exit strategies to protect profits and minimise losses in various market environments.

- **Preventing premature exits:** Using volatility-based exits can help traders avoid being stopped out of a position prematurely due to short-term price fluctuations.

- **Providing dynamic exit levels:** Volatility-based exits adjust exit levels as market conditions change, helping traders maintain an appropriate level of risk throughout the duration of a trade.

Advantages and Disadvantages of Using Volatility-based Exits

Advantages

- **Market adaptability:** Volatility-based exits allow traders to adjust their exit strategies according to current market conditions, enhancing the effectiveness of their risk management approach.

- **Dynamic exit levels:** By accounting for changes in volatility, traders can maintain appropriate exit levels throughout the duration of a trade.

- **Reduced likelihood of premature exits:** Volatility-based exits consider short-term price fluctuations, reducing the chances of being stopped out of a position too early.

Disadvantages

- **Complexity:** Incorporating volatility measures into exit strategies can be more complex than using static exit levels, potentially making it more challenging for some traders to implement effectively.

- **Potential for increased risk:** If not managed correctly, volatility-based exits could result in traders taking on more risk than intended, particularly in highly volatile markets.

- **Reliance on historical volatility:** Volatility measures are typically based on historical data, which may not accurately predict future market conditions or price fluctuations.

Best Practices for Implementing Volatility-based Exits in Different Market Conditions

- **Combine with other exit strategies:** Use volatility-based exits in conjunction with other exit techniques, such as technical indicator-based exits or time-based exits, to create a comprehensive trade management system.

- **Adjust parameters:** Fine-tune the parameters of your volatility measures to suit your trading style, risk tolerance, and the current market conditions.

- **Regularly review and update:** Continuously monitor your volatility-based exit strategies and make adjustments as necessary to maintain an effective risk management approach.

- **Understand the limitations:** Recognize the limitations of relying solely on volatility-based exits and consider other factors, such as market context, fundamentals, and technical analysis, when making trading decisions.

Moving Average Crossovers

Definition and Explanation

Moving average crossovers are a technical analysis technique that involves comparing two different moving averages to identify potential trade entry and exit points. A moving average is a lagging indicator that smooths out price data to identify trends and reduce noise. When a shorter-term moving average crosses above or below a longer-term moving average, it can signal a change in the prevailing trend and serve as a trade management tool.

Using Moving Average Crossovers as a Trade Management Tool

Moving average crossovers can be used as a trade management tool in several ways:

- **Trade Entry:** A moving average crossover can signal a potential trade entry when the shorter-term moving average crosses above the longer-term moving average, indicating a potential uptrend. Conversely, a crossover below the longer-term moving average may signal a potential downtrend and a short trade entry.

- **Trade Exit:** Traders can use moving average crossovers to exit trades when the shorter-term moving average crosses back below or above the longer-term moving average, suggesting that the trend may be reversing.

- **Stop Loss Adjustments:** As the moving averages change over time, traders can adjust their stop loss levels to follow the moving averages, protecting profits and minimising risk.

The Role of Moving Average Crossovers in Risk Management

Moving average crossovers can play a significant role in risk management by:

- **Identifying Trend Changes:** Moving average crossovers can help traders identify potential trend reversals, allowing them to exit trades before the market moves against them.
- **Dynamic Stop Losses:** By using moving average crossovers to adjust stop loss levels, traders can protect their profits and minimise risk in changing market conditions.
- **Reducing Emotional Bias:** Moving average crossovers provide a systematic approach to trade management, helping traders make decisions based on objective data rather than emotions.

Advantages and Disadvantages of Using Moving Average Crossovers

Advantages:

- **Trend Identification:** Moving average crossovers can help traders identify and follow prevailing market trends, potentially improving trade outcomes.

- **Systematic Approach:** Moving average crossovers provide an objective, data-driven method for managing trades, reducing the impact of emotional biases.

- **Versatility:** Traders can customise moving average crossovers by choosing different timeframes and types of moving averages to suit their trading style and market conditions.

Disadvantages:

- **Lagging Indicator:** Since moving averages are lagging indicators, moving average crossovers may sometimes generate late signals, causing traders to miss optimal entry or exit points.

- **False Signals:** Moving average crossovers can generate false signals in sideways or choppy markets, leading to whipsaw trades and potential losses.

- **Inefficiency:** In some cases, other trade management strategies, such as trailing stops or profit targets, may be more effective in specific market conditions.

Best Practices for Implementing Moving Average Crossovers in Different Market Conditions

- Choose the appropriate moving averages and timeframes for your trading style and the prevailing market conditions. Experiment with different combinations to find the most effective settings for your strategy.

- Combine moving average crossovers with other technical analysis tools, such as support and resistance levels, trend lines, or chart patterns, to improve the accuracy of trade signals and enhance risk management.

- Be aware of the limitations of moving average crossovers and avoid relying solely on this technique for trade management. Incorporate other risk management strategies, such as stop loss orders and position sizing, to create a comprehensive trading plan.

- Monitor the performance of your moving average crossover strategy and make adjustments as necessary to optimise trade outcomes and risk management.

- Stay disciplined and consistently apply your moving average crossover strategy across all trades to ensure long-term success.

- Be cautious when using moving average crossovers in choppy or sideways markets, as they may generate false signals. Consider using additional filters or switching to a range-bound trading strategy in such market conditions.

- Adjust your moving average settings to account for changing market volatility. For example, in more volatile markets, consider using shorter moving average timeframes to capture shorter-term trends and avoid late signals.

- Backtest your moving average crossover strategy on historical price data to evaluate its effectiveness and make necessary adjustments before implementing it in live trading.

- Use proper risk management techniques, such as position sizing and stop loss orders, to protect your trading capital and minimise the impact of losing trades.

Technical Indicator-based Exits

Definition and Explanation

Technical indicator-based exits are trade management techniques that use technical indicators to signal when a trader should exit a position. These indicators help traders determine optimal exit points based on changes in market conditions, trends, or momentum. Some common technical indicators used for exit signals include the Relative Strength Index (RSI), Moving Average Convergence Divergence (MACD), and Bollinger Bands.

Using Technical Indicators to Signal Exits

- **RSI:** The Relative Strength Index measures the momentum of price movements, with overbought and oversold levels typically indicating potential reversals. Traders may exit a position when the RSI reaches an overbought or oversold level, suggesting that the trend may be losing momentum or reversing.

- **MACD:** The Moving Average Convergence Divergence indicator helps identify changes in momentum by comparing short-term and long-term moving averages. Traders may exit a position when the MACD line crosses above or below the signal line, indicating a potential change in momentum or trend direction.

- **Bollinger Bands:** Bollinger Bands measure price volatility by plotting two standard deviations above and below a moving average. Traders may exit a position when the price touches the upper or lower band, suggesting that the price may be overextended and due for a reversal or consolidation.

The Role of Technical Indicator-based Exits in Risk Management

Technical indicator-based exits play a vital role in risk management by:

- **Providing objective exit signals:** By relying on technical indicators, traders can remove emotion and subjectivity from the decision-making process, leading to more consistent and disciplined trade management.

- **Protecting profits:** Using technical indicators to signal exits can help traders protect their profits by identifying when a trend or momentum may be weakening or reversing.

- **Minimising losses:** When a trade moves against a trader's expectations, technical indicators can provide early exit signals, allowing traders to minimise their losses.

Advantages and Disadvantages of Using Technical Indicator-based Exits

Advantages:

- **Objective signals:** Technical indicator-based exits provide objective signals based on mathematical calculations, reducing the influence of emotions and subjectivity.

- **Adaptable to different market conditions:** Technical indicators can be applied to various market conditions, allowing traders to adjust their exit strategies accordingly.

- **Customizable:** Traders can fine-tune the parameters of technical indicators to suit their trading style and preferences.

Disadvantages:

- **False signals:** Technical indicators can sometimes generate false exit signals, causing traders to exit profitable positions prematurely or hold onto losing positions for too long.

- **Lagging nature:** Some technical indicators are lagging, meaning they generate exit signals after the fact, potentially causing traders to miss optimal exit points.

- **Overreliance on a single indicator:** Relying solely on a single technical indicator for exit signals may not provide a comprehensive view of the market and can lead to suboptimal trade management decisions.

Best Practices for Implementing Technical Indicator-based Exits in Different Market Conditions

- **Combine multiple indicators:** Use a combination of technical indicators to generate exit signals, reducing the likelihood of false signals and increasing the robustness of your exit strategy.

- **Adjust indicator parameters:** Fine-tune the parameters of technical indicators to suit your trading style, risk tolerance, and the current market conditions.

- **Test and evaluate:** Regularly backtest and evaluate the performance of your technical indicator-based exit strategies, making adjustments as needed to improve their effectiveness.

- **Integrate with other trade management techniques:** Combine technical indicator-based exits with other trade management tools, such as stop-loss orders and trailing stops, to create a comprehensive risk management plan.

By incorporating technical indicator-based exits into your trade management strategy, you can improve your ability to protect profits and minimise losses in various market conditions.

However, it is essential to recognize the limitations of relying solely on technical indicators for exit signals and to consider other factors, such as market context, fundamentals, and risk tolerance, to make well-informed trading decisions.

Definition and Explanation

Inter market analysis is a method of analysing the relationships between different asset classes or financial markets, such as stocks, bonds, commodities, and currencies. By examining these relationships, traders can gain insights into market trends, potential reversals, and correlations that can influence their trading decisions. Inter market analysis exits refer to trade management strategies that involve exiting a position based on developments or changes in related markets.

Managing Trades Based on Inter market Analysis

- **Correlations:** Identifying correlations between asset classes and using them to manage trade exits. For example, if a trader observes that a specific currency pair and a commodity have a strong inverse correlation, they may decide to exit a position in one market if the other market signals a reversal.

- **Divergences:** Monitoring divergences between related markets to identify potential trend reversals or weakening trends, which may trigger trade exits. For example, if a trader notices that the stock market is rising but the bond market is not falling as expected, they may exit a long position in stocks based on the potential for a trend reversal.

- **Market breadth:** Assessing the overall strength or weakness of a market by analysing the performance of related markets or sectors. Traders may choose to exit a position if related markets show signs of deteriorating strength or increasing weakness.

The Role of Inter Market Analysis Exits in Risk Management

- **Diversification:** Using inter market analysis to manage trade exits can help traders diversify their risk by considering information from multiple markets.

- **Market context:** Inter market analysis provides a broader context for understanding market behaviour, which can help traders make more informed decisions about when to exit a position.

- **Early warning signals:** Analysing related markets can help traders identify early warning signals for potential trend reversals or market shifts, allowing them to exit positions before significant losses occur.

Advantages and Disadvantages of Using Inter Market Analysis Exits

Advantages

- **Broader perspective:** Inter market analysis provides a more comprehensive view of market trends and conditions, which can help traders make better-informed exit decisions.

- **Enhanced risk management:** By considering information from multiple markets, traders can potentially reduce their risk exposure and improve the overall performance of their trading strategies.

- **Early warning signals:** Inter market analysis can help traders identify early warning signals for potential market shifts or trend reversals, allowing them to exit positions before significant losses occur.

Disadvantage

- **Complexity:** Inter market analysis can be complex and require a deep understanding of various asset classes and their relationships.

- **False signals:** Inter market relationships can change over time, and relying on these relationships for trade exits can sometimes result in false signals or premature exits.

- **Overemphasis on correlations:** While correlations can be useful in inter market analysis, traders should be cautious not to overemphasise their importance or rely solely on them for trade management decisions.

Best Practices for Implementing Inter Market Analysis Exits in Different Market Conditions

- **Stay informed:** Regularly monitor and analyse developments in related markets to stay up-to-date on trends and correlations that may impact your trading decisions.

- **Use multiple analysis tools:** Combine inter market analysis with other technical and fundamental analysis techniques to make more informed trade exit decisions.

- **Diversify strategies:** Incorporate inter market analysis exits alongside other trade management strategies to create a more robust and diversified approach to risk management.

- **Adjust to market conditions:** Be prepared to adjust your inter market analysis strategies as market conditions and relationships between asset classes change.

- **Validate relationships:** Regularly assess the validity of the relationships between markets and adjust your strategies accordingly to ensure they remain effective.

Multiple Timeframe Analysis Exits

Definition and Explanation

Multiple timeframe analysis involves examining and analysing the same financial instrument or market on different timeframes, such as daily, weekly, and monthly charts. This technique helps traders identify trends, support and resistance levels, and potential reversals across various timeframes. Multiple timeframe analysis exits refer to trade management strategies that involve exiting a position based on signals or developments observed in different timeframes.

Using Analysis from Multiple Timeframes to Manage Trades

- **Trend confirmation:** Analysing multiple timeframes can help traders confirm the direction of the prevailing trend, which can influence their decisions on when to exit a trade.

- **Reversal signals:** Examining different timeframes can help traders spot potential trend reversals, allowing them to exit a position before the market moves against them.

- **Support and resistance levels:** Identifying key support and resistance levels across various timeframes can help traders determine appropriate exit points for their trades.

The Role of Multiple Timeframe Analysis Exits in Risk Management

- **Improved trade timing:** By analysing multiple timeframes, traders can potentially improve their trade timing, which can help reduce the risk of entering or exiting a trade at an unfavourable price.

- **Enhanced trend analysis:** Examining different timeframes can provide a more comprehensive understanding of market trends, allowing traders to make better-informed decisions about when to exit a position.

- **Diversification:** Using multiple timeframe analysis can help traders diversify their risk by considering information from different timeframes, reducing the likelihood of making decisions based on short-term market noise.

Advantages and Disadvantages of Using Multiple Timeframe Analysis Exits

Advantages

- **Comprehensive analysis:** Multiple timeframe analysis provides a more in-depth understanding of market trends and potential reversals, which can help traders make better-informed decisions about when to exit a trade.

- **Flexibility:** Multiple timeframe analysis exits can be applied to various trading strategies and market conditions, making them a versatile trade management tool.

- **Reduced risk:** By considering multiple timeframes, traders can potentially reduce the risk of making decisions based on short-term market noise or temporary fluctuations.

Disadvantages

- **Complexity:** Analysing multiple timeframes can be more complex and time-consuming than focusing on a single timeframe.

- **Conflicting signals:** Traders may sometimes encounter conflicting signals from different timeframes, which can make it challenging to decide on the appropriate exit strategy.

- **Over-analysis:** There is a risk of over-analysing the market when using multiple timeframe analysis, leading to indecision or delayed trade execution.

Best Practices for Implementing Multiple Timeframe Analysis Exits in Different Market Conditions

- **Start with a higher timeframe:** Begin your analysis with a higher timeframe to gain a broader perspective of the market trend and potential support and resistance levels.

- **Narrow down to lower timeframes:** Once you have a clear understanding of the higher timeframe, move to lower timeframes to refine your exit levels and identify more precise signals.

- **Prioritise signals from higher timeframes**: In the case of conflicting signals, prioritise those from higher timeframes, as they often carry more weight and provide a more accurate representation of the prevailing trend.

- **Use a combination of technical tools:** Supplement your multiple timeframe analysis with other technical tools, such as trendlines, moving averages, and oscillators, to confirm your exit signals and enhance your trade management strategy.

Sentiment Analysis Exits

Definition and Explanation

Sentiment analysis exits are trade management techniques that rely on the analysis of market sentiment to determine when to exit or adjust positions. Sentiment analysis involves the assessment of the collective opinions, emotions, and attitudes of market participants towards a particular asset or market. This information is often derived from sources like social media, news articles, and market research.

Using Sentiment Analysis to Manage Trades

- **Social Media Sentiment**: Traders can analyse social media platforms such as Twitter, Reddit, or StockTwits to gauge the sentiment of market participants and adjust positions accordingly.

- **News Sentiment:** Analysing the tone and content of news articles can help traders identify shifts in market sentiment that may influence asset prices.

- **Sentiment Indicators:** Some technical indicators, such as the Fear & Greed Index or the Put/Call Ratio, can provide insights into market sentiment and be used to manage trades.

The Role of Sentiment Analysis Exits in Risk Management

Sentiment analysis exits can play a crucial role in risk management by:

- **Detecting shifts in market sentiment:** Identifying changes in sentiment can help traders anticipate potential market reversals or trend continuations.

- **Reducing emotional bias:** Using sentiment analysis to inform exit decisions can help traders avoid making impulsive or emotionally driven decisions.

- **Providing additional confirmation:** Sentiment analysis can be used in conjunction with other technical or fundamental analysis tools to confirm exit signals and increase the likelihood of successful trade management.

Advantages and Disadvantages of Using Sentiment Analysis Exits

Advantages:

- **Early detection of sentiment shifts:** Sentiment analysis can help traders identify changes in market sentiment before they are reflected in asset prices.

- **Diversification of information sources:** Analysing sentiment from various sources can provide traders with a more comprehensive understanding of market dynamics.

- **Complementary to other analysis techniques:** Sentiment analysis can be used in combination with other technical or fundamental analysis tools to improve the overall effectiveness of trade management strategies.

Disadvantages:

- **Subjectivity:** Sentiment analysis can be subjective, and different traders may interpret sentiment data differently, leading to inconsistencies in trade management.

- **Noisy data:** Social media and news sources can contain a significant amount of noise, making it challenging to identify genuine sentiment signals.

- **Time-consuming:** Conducting sentiment analysis can be time-consuming, particularly for traders who manually analyse large volumes of data.

Best Practices for Implementing Sentiment Analysis Exits in Different Market Conditions

- **Use multiple sentiment sources:** Analyse sentiment data from various sources, such as social media, news articles, and sentiment indicators, to get a more comprehensive view of market sentiment.

- **Filter noise:** Develop strategies for filtering out irrelevant or misleading information and focus on reliable sentiment signals.

- **Combine sentiment analysis with other techniques:** Use sentiment analysis in conjunction with other technical or fundamental analysis tools to improve the accuracy of exit signals.

- **Monitor sentiment data regularly:** Stay up-to-date with sentiment data to detect shifts in market sentiment promptly and adjust positions accordingly.

Market Internals-based Exits

Market internals-based exits refer to trade management strategies that rely on market internals to inform exit decisions. Market internals are measures of the overall health and direction of the market, providing insights into the underlying strength or weakness of market trends. Examples of market internals include market breadth, advance-decline line, new highs and new lows, and volume-based indicators.

Using Market Internals to Manage Trades

- **Market breadth:** Market breadth indicators, such as the advance-decline ratio or the percentage of stocks above their moving averages, can provide insights into the strength of a market trend and help determine whether to hold or exit a trade.

- **Advance-decline line:** The advance-decline line measures the net advances (advancing issues minus declining issues) and can help identify trend reversals, which may signal an exit opportunity.

- **New highs and new lows:** Monitoring the number of stocks making new highs or new lows can indicate market strength or weakness, informing exit decisions.

- **Volume-based indicators:** Indicators such as the up-down volume ratio or the Arms Index (TRIN) can provide insights into the balance between buying and selling pressure in the market, helping traders decide when to exit a trade.

The Role of Market Internals-based Exits in Risk Management

- **Identifying trend reversals:** Market internals can help traders identify potential trend reversals, allowing them to exit positions before significant losses occur.

- **Confirming market strength or weakness:** Using market internals to confirm the strength or weakness of a market trend can help traders manage risk by exiting trades in unfavourable conditions or holding trades in favourable conditions.

- **Diversification:** Market internals-based exits provide an alternative exit strategy to traditional technical or fundamental analysis, diversifying risk management techniques.

Advantages and Disadvantages of Using Market Internals-based Exits

Advantages:

- **Broad market perspective:** Market internals provide a comprehensive view of the market's overall health, which can help traders make better-informed exit decisions.

- **Early warning signals:** Market internals can help identify potential trend reversals or periods of market weakness before they become apparent in price action, allowing traders to exit positions earlier and reduce risk.

- **Complementary tool:** Market internals-based exits can complement other trade management strategies, providing a more robust approach to risk management.

Disadvantages:

- **Lagging indicators:** Some market internals, such as moving averages or cumulative indicators, can be lagging, potentially delaying exit signals and increasing risk.

- **False signals:** Market internals can sometimes provide false signals, leading traders to exit positions prematurely or hold onto losing trades.

- **Complexity:** Interpreting market internals and incorporating them into trade management strategies can be complex and require a solid understanding of market mechanics.

Best Practices for Implementing Market Internals-based Exits in Different Market Conditions

- **Combine with other strategies:** Use market internals-based exits in conjunction with other trade management strategies, such as technical analysis or fundamental analysis, to improve the overall effectiveness of risk management.

- **Use multiple market internals:** Incorporate a variety of market internals to gain a more comprehensive view of the market and reduce the likelihood of false signals.

- **Monitor changes in market internals:** Continuously monitor market internals to identify shifts in market conditions and adjust exit strategies accordingly.

- **Develop a clear exit plan:** Establish specific criteria based on market internals for exiting trades and stick to the plan to maintain discipline and minimise emotional decision-making.

- **Adapt to different market conditions:** Understand how different market conditions can affect the reliability of market internals and adjust exit strategies accordingly.

Fundamental Analysis Exits

Definition and Explanation

Fundamental analysis exits are trade management techniques that use fundamental factors, such as earnings reports, economic data, and other company or macroeconomic information, to determine when to exit a trade. This approach focuses on the underlying value and financial health of an asset rather than relying solely on price action or technical indicators.

Using Fundamental Analysis to Manage Trades

- **Earnings Reports:** Traders can use earnings reports to gauge a company's performance, and if the results significantly deviate from expectations, they might decide to exit or adjust their position.

- **Economic Data:** Economic indicators, such as employment data, GDP growth, or inflation rates, can influence market trends and asset prices. Traders might use this information to adjust their trades accordingly.

- **News and Events:** Significant news events or announcements, such as mergers, acquisitions, or regulatory changes, can impact the value of a financial asset, and traders can use these events as exit signals.

The Role of Fundamental Analysis Exits in Risk Management

Fundamental analysis exits play a significant role in risk management by:

- **Providing a broader perspective:** Incorporating fundamental analysis into exit strategies offers a more comprehensive understanding of the factors influencing asset prices, complementing technical analysis and market context.

- **Anticipating market trends:** By monitoring and analysing fundamental factors, traders can anticipate shifts in market trends and adjust their positions accordingly, potentially reducing risk and protecting profits.

- **Aligning trades with long-term value:** Focusing on the underlying value of an asset ensures that trades are aligned with long-term fundamentals, reducing the likelihood of being swayed by short-term market fluctuations.

Advantages and Disadvantages of Using Fundamental Analysis Exits

Advantages:

- **Comprehensive perspective:** Fundamental analysis provides a broader understanding of the factors influencing asset prices, allowing traders to make more informed decisions.

- **Long-term focus:** By focusing on the underlying value of an asset, traders can potentially achieve more stable returns over the long run.

- **Anticipating market shifts:** Monitoring fundamental factors can help traders anticipate and respond to changes in market trends.

Disadvantages:

- **Time-consuming:** Conducting thorough fundamental analysis can be time-consuming and may require extensive knowledge of financial markets, economics, and accounting principles.

- **Subjectivity:** Fundamental analysis involves interpreting qualitative information, which can be subjective and open to different interpretations.

- **Limited short-term application:** Fundamental analysis is typically more useful for long-term investing rather than short-term trading, as it may not accurately reflect short-term price fluctuations.

Best Practices for Implementing Fundamental Analysis Exits in Different Market Conditions

- **Combine with technical analysis:** Use fundamental analysis in conjunction with technical analysis to create a comprehensive trading approach that accounts for both underlying value and price action.

- **Stay informed:** Regularly monitor economic data releases, earnings reports, and news events to stay updated on the factors influencing the assets you trade.

- **Set clear exit criteria:** Establish specific fundamental criteria that will trigger an exit, such as a change in earnings growth, a shift in macroeconomic conditions, or a significant news event.

- **Adapt to market conditions:** Recognize that different market conditions may require different approaches to fundamental analysis, and adjust your exit strategies accordingly.

News-based Exits

Definition and Explanation

News-based exits are trade management techniques that use market-moving news and events as triggers for exiting or adjusting positions. This approach acknowledges the potential impact of significant news on asset prices and allows traders to react quickly to changes in market sentiment.

Managing Trades Based on Market-moving News and Events

- **Scheduled News Releases:** Economic data releases, earnings reports, and central bank announcements are examples of scheduled news events that can impact financial markets. Traders can monitor these events and adjust their positions accordingly.

- **Unscheduled News:** Unexpected news, such as natural disasters, geopolitical events, or company-specific announcements, can cause sudden market volatility. Traders should remain vigilant and have plans in place to respond to unscheduled news events.

- **Sentiment Shifts:** News can cause shifts in market sentiment, leading to changes in asset prices. Traders can use news-based exits to respond to sentiment shifts and protect their positions.

The Role of News-based Exits in Risk Management

News-based exits play a significant role in risk management by:

- **Allowing for quick reactions:** News-based exits enable traders to respond quickly to market-moving news, potentially limiting losses and protecting profits.

- **Enhancing situational awareness:** Monitoring news events helps traders stay informed about the factors influencing the markets, enabling them to make better-informed decisions.

- **Mitigating event risk:** Exiting or adjusting positions in response to news events can help traders manage event risk and reduce the likelihood of being caught off guard by unexpected developments.

Advantages and Disadvantages of Using News-based Exits

Advantages:

- **Rapid response:** News-based exits allow traders to act quickly in response to market-moving news, potentially limiting losses and protecting profits.

- **Enhanced market understanding:** Monitoring news events provides traders with valuable insights into market dynamics and helps them stay informed about the factors driving asset prices.

- **Adaptability:** News-based exits can be applied across various market conditions and asset classes, making them a versatile trade management tool.

Disadvantages:

- **Increased volatility:** News events can cause significant market volatility, which may result in higher trading costs and increased risk.

- **False signals:** Not all news events have a lasting impact on asset prices, and reacting to every news event may lead to unnecessary trade adjustments.

- **Emotional bias:** Traders may become emotionally attached to news events, leading to impulsive decisions and suboptimal trade management.

Best Practices for Implementing News-based Exits in Different Market Conditions

- **Prioritise significant news:** Focus on news events with a high potential for market impact, and avoid overreacting to minor or irrelevant news.

- **Set clear exit criteria:** Establish specific news-based criteria that will trigger an exit or position adjustment, and stick to these rules to avoid emotional decision-making.

- **Monitor multiple news sources:** Stay informed by following various news sources, including financial news websites, social media, and market analysis reports.

- **Remain adaptable:** Recognize that different market conditions may require different news-based exit strategies and be prepared to adjust your approach accordingly.

Chapter - Enhancing Your Strategy

Pyramiding into Additional Trades

Definition and Explanation

Pyramiding is a trade management strategy in which traders increase their position size as the market moves in their favour. By adding to a winning trade, traders can potentially amplify their gains while maintaining the original risk level. Pyramiding can be implemented through various methods, such as scaling in and scaling out strategies.

Scaling In and Scaling Out Strategies

Scaling In: Scaling in involves gradually increasing position size as the market moves in the trader's favour. This can be done by adding new positions at predetermined price levels or based on specific technical indicators. Scaling in allows traders to capitalise on a trend by increasing exposure as the market continues to move in their favour.

Scaling Out: Scaling out is the opposite of scaling in, where traders gradually reduce their position size as the market moves in their favour. This can help traders lock in profits while still maintaining some exposure to the market for potential further gains. Scaling out can be implemented by closing a portion of the position at predetermined profit targets or based on specific technical indicators.

The Role of Pyramiding in Risk Management

Pyramiding plays a crucial role in risk management by:

- **Maximising Potential Gains:** By adding to winning trades, pyramiding can help traders amplify their gains while maintaining the original risk level.

- **Risk Control:** When properly implemented, pyramiding strategies maintain the original risk level by adding new positions without increasing the overall risk exposure. This can be achieved by adjusting stop loss levels or position sizes accordingly.

- **Diversifying Risk:** Pyramiding strategies can help traders diversify risk across multiple entry points, reducing the impact of adverse price movements on a single position.

Advantages and Disadvantages of Using Pyramiding Strategies

Advantages:

- Potentially amplifies gains in winning trades.

- Maintains the original risk level when properly implemented.

- Diversifies risk across multiple entry points.

Disadvantages:

- Requires accurate market analysis and timing to identify favourable entry points.

- May lead to overexposure if not properly managed, increasing the overall risk.

- May not be suitable for all types of trading strategies or market conditions.

Best Practices for Implementing Pyramiding in Different Market Conditions

- Use a combination of technical and fundamental analysis to identify strong trends and favourable entry points for pyramiding.

- Set clear rules for adding and exiting positions, such as pre-determined price levels or technical indicators.

- Adjust stop loss levels and position sizes accordingly when adding new positions to maintain the original risk level.

- Monitor market conditions and adjust pyramiding strategies as needed. For example, consider scaling out of positions in more volatile markets or when the trend shows signs of weakening.

- Combine pyramiding strategies with other risk management techniques, such as stop loss orders or profit targets, to optimise trade outcomes.

Comparison of Pyramiding and Inverse Pyramiding Risk-Return

Pyramiding: Pyramiding involves adding to winning trades, potentially amplifying gains while maintaining the original risk level. This strategy generally results in a higher return potential as the market moves in the trader's favour. However, it requires accurate market analysis and timing to implement effectively.

Inverse Pyramiding: Inverse pyramiding involves adding to losing trades, typically with the expectation that the market will eventually reverse in the trader's favour. This strategy can result in higher losses if the market continues to move against the trader. While inverse pyramiding can potentially lead to higher returns if the market reverses, it generally carries a higher risk level than standard pyramiding strategies.

By understanding the benefits and drawbacks of pyramiding and inverse pyramiding strategies, traders can make informed decisions about which approach best suits their risk tolerance and trading objectives. It is essential to carefully consider market conditions, trading strategy, and risk management techniques when implementing these strategies.

Option-based Strategies

Definition and Explanation

Option-based strategies involve using options, such as calls and puts, as a trade management tool. Options are financial derivatives that give the buyer the right, but not the obligation, to buy or sell an underlying asset at a predetermined price on or before a specific date. Traders can use option-based strategies to hedge positions, generate income, or protect against potential losses.

Using Options to Manage Trades (e.g., Protective Puts, Covered Calls)

- **Protective Puts:** A protective put strategy involves purchasing a put option on an asset that a trader already owns. This approach provides a downside protection, as the put option increases in value if the asset's price declines, offsetting potential losses on the underlying position.

- **Covered Calls:** A covered call strategy involves owning an asset and selling call options on that same asset. This approach generates income through the premium received from selling the call options. However, it also caps the potential upside, as the trader is obligated to sell the asset at the strike price if the call options are exercised.

The Role of Option-based Strategies in Risk Management

Option-based strategies can play a crucial role in risk management by:

- **Providing Downside Protection:** Protective puts offer a hedge against potential losses on an underlying asset.

- **Generating Income:** Covered call strategies can provide an additional income stream for traders, helping to offset potential losses or enhance overall returns.

- **Enhancing Portfolio Diversification:** Options can be used to create various risk and return profiles, allowing traders to diversify their portfolios and manage risk more effectively.

Advantages and Disadvantages of Using Option-based Strategies

Advantages:

- **Risk Management:** Option-based strategies can provide downside protection and income generation, helping to manage risk more effectively.

- **Flexibility:** Options offer a wide range of possible strategies, allowing traders to tailor their approach to suit their risk tolerance and market outlook.

- **Diversification:** Option-based strategies can diversify a trader's portfolio and improve overall risk management.

Disadvantages:

- **Costs:** Trading options involves additional costs, such as commissions and bid-ask spreads, which can reduce overall returns.

- **Complexity:** Option-based strategies can be more complex than other trade management techniques, requiring a deeper understanding of options and their associated risks.

- **Limited Gains:** Some option-based strategies, such as covered calls, can limit potential gains if the underlying asset's price increases significantly.

Best Practices for Implementing Option-based Strategies in Different Market Conditions

- **Educate Yourself:** Gain a solid understanding of options, their pricing, and the various strategies available before implementing option-based trade management techniques.

- **Assess Your Risk Tolerance:** Determine your risk tolerance and trading objectives before selecting an appropriate option-based strategy.

- **Monitor Market Conditions:** Keep an eye on market conditions and adjust your option-based strategies accordingly to optimise risk management and potential returns.

- **Manage Costs:** Be mindful of the costs associated with trading options and factor them into your overall risk management and profit expectations.

- **Combine Option-based Strategies with Other Techniques:** Use option-based strategies in conjunction with other trade management tools and techniques to create a comprehensive risk management plan.

Algorithmic Trade Management

Definition and Explanation

Algorithmic trade management refers to the use of computer algorithms and automated trading systems to manage trades based on predefined rules, strategies, and conditions. This approach to trade management allows for greater precision, speed, and consistency in executing trade management strategies compared to manual methods. Algorithmic trade management can include a wide range of strategies, from simple stop-loss orders to more complex, adaptive systems that adjust trade management decisions based on real-time market data and conditions.

Using Algorithmic Trade Management Strategies

- **Automated stop-loss and take-profit orders:** Implementing algorithmic systems to automatically place and adjust stop-loss and take-profit orders based on predetermined rules.

- **Dynamic position sizing:** Using algorithms to adjust position sizes based on market volatility, risk tolerance, and other factors.

- **Adaptive trailing stops:** Developing algorithms to adapt trailing stop distances based on market conditions, such as volatility or trend strength.

- **Time-based exits:** Automating trade exits based on pre-determined holding periods or specific times of day.

- **Technical indicator-based exits:** Implementing algorithmic systems to exit trades based on signals from technical indicators, such as moving average crossovers or RSI levels.

The Role of Algorithmic Trade Management in Risk Management

- **Speed and precision:** Algorithmic trade management allows for faster and more precise execution of trade management strategies, minimising slippage and reducing risk.

- **Consistency:** Automated trade management ensures consistent application of strategies, reducing the impact of emotions and human error on decision-making.

- **Customization:** Algorithmic systems can be tailored to individual trading styles and risk tolerances, allowing for more effective risk management.

- **Adaptability:** Advanced algorithmic systems can adapt to changing market conditions, improving the effectiveness of trade management strategies in various market environments.

Advantages and Disadvantages of Using Algorithmic Trade Management

Advantages:

- **Speed:** Algorithmic trade management enables rapid execution of strategies, reducing the impact of market fluctuations on trade outcomes.

- **Consistency:** Automated systems help maintain discipline and consistency in trade management, minimising the effects of emotions and human error.

- **Customization:** Traders can develop and fine-tune algorithmic systems to suit their specific trading styles and risk preferences.

- **Adaptability:** Advanced algorithms can adapt to changing market conditions, improving the effectiveness of trade management strategies.

Disadvantages:

- **Over-optimization:** Algorithmic systems can be overly optimised for specific market conditions, leading to poor performance when market conditions change.

- **Technical complexity:** Developing and maintaining algorithmic trade management systems requires advanced technical knowledge and skills.

- **Dependency on technology:** Relying on algorithmic systems introduces the risk of technical issues or failures, which can impact trade management and overall performance.

- **Reduced flexibility:** Automated systems can lack the flexibility to adapt to unique market situations or take advantage of unexpected opportunities.

Best Practices for Implementing Algorithmic Trade Management in Different Market Conditions

- **Develop robust strategies**: Ensure algorithmic systems are based on sound trading principles and strategies, not over-optimized for specific market conditions.

- **Test and validate:** Thoroughly backtest and validate algorithmic systems using historical data and forward testing to ensure their effectiveness across a range of market conditions.

- **Monitor performance:** Continuously monitor the performance of algorithmic systems, making adjustments and updates as necessary to maintain their effectiveness.

- **Maintain flexibility:** Combine algorithmic trade management with discretionary decision-making to maintain flexibility and adaptability in different market situations.

- **Diversify strategies:** Use a combination of algorithmic and non-algorithmic trade management strategies to reduce dependency on any single approach and enhance overall risk management.

Position Sizing and Risk Management

Position sizing is a critical aspect of trading that determines the number of shares, contracts, or units to trade for a given position. It plays a significant role in risk management, as it helps to protect a trader's capital by limiting potential losses. Proper position sizing can also improve the overall performance of a trading strategy by helping traders achieve their desired risk-reward ratio.

The Importance of Position Sizing in Trade Management

- Position sizing is essential for several reasons. First and foremost, it helps traders manage their risk by controlling the size of their trades, which directly affects the potential gains and losses. It also ensures that traders do not overexpose themselves to a particular asset, sector, or market, which can lead to significant losses if the market moves against their positions. Furthermore, position sizing helps traders maintain emotional stability by preventing them from risking too much on any single trade, which can lead to impulsive decision-making and poor trade execution.

Proper position sizing is essential for effective trade management, as it helps traders:

- Maintain discipline by preventing overtrading or undertrading.

- Preserve capital by limiting the impact of individual trade losses on the overall account.

- Achieve a better risk-reward ratio by aligning trade size with the potential gains and losses.

Comprehensive Risk Assessment

Risk Tolerance

Risk tolerance is a crucial factor in position sizing and risk management, as it refers to the level of risk a trader is willing to accept. Traders can have varying risk tolerance levels, from conservative to aggressive. Conservative traders are more risk-averse and prioritise protecting their capital, while aggressive traders are more willing to take risks for potentially higher returns. Understanding one's risk tolerance is vital in determining the appropriate position size and managing risk effectively.

Capital at Risk

Capital at risk is the amount of money a trader is willing to lose on a single trade. This factor is essential in determining the appropriate position size, as it helps traders manage their losses and protect their trading accounts. By setting a limit on the capital at risk for each trade, traders can control their potential losses and ensure they don't jeopardise their entire account balance.

Allocating a specific portion of the account balance for each trade ensures that traders remain disciplined and focused on their risk management strategy.

Maximum Drawdown

Maximum drawdown is the most significant drop in account value that a trader experiences during a specific period. Monitoring maximum drawdown is important because it can help traders identify potential issues with their trading strategies and make adjustments to reduce risk and improve performance. By analysing drawdowns, traders can gain insights into the effectiveness of their risk management and position sizing strategies. This information can be used to make necessary adjustments, such as reducing position size during periods of high volatility or when trading less liquid assets, to minimise the risk of substantial losses.

Techniques for Determining Optimal Position Size

There are several techniques for determining optimal position size, including:

Fixed Dollar Amount

- **Description:** The Fixed Dollar Amount method involves risking a constant dollar amount per trade, regardless of account size or asset volatility. This method is straightforward to implement but may not be the most efficient in terms of risk management.

- **Example**: A trader decides to risk $1,000 per trade, irrespective of the account size or the volatility of the asset being traded.

Fixed Percentage

- **Description:** The Fixed Percentage method involves risking a constant percentage of the account equity per trade. This approach automatically adjusts the position size based on the trader's account balance, providing better risk management than the fixed dollar amount method.

- **Example:** A trader decides to risk 2% of their account equity per trade. If the account balance is $50,000, the trader would risk $1,000 (2% of $50,000) on each trade.

Fixed Fractional

- **Description:** The Fixed Fractional method involves risking a percentage of account equity per unit of expected loss. This approach takes into account both the account balance and the expected loss, providing a more dynamic risk management strategy.

- **Example:** A trader decides to risk 0.5% of their account equity per $1,000 of expected loss. If the trader's account balance is $100,000 and the expected loss on a trade is $2,000, the trader would risk 1% ($1,000) on that trade.

Fixed Ratio

- **Description:** The Fixed Ratio method uses a fixed dollar amount per unit of risk, such as per 1% drawdown. This approach adjusts the position size based on the level of risk taken and can be more conservative than other methods.

- **Example:** A trader decides to risk $500 for every 1% drawdown. If a trade has an expected drawdown of 2%, the trader would risk $1,000 ($500 x 2) on the trade.

Kelly Criterion

- **Description:** The Kelly Criterion is a formula used to calculate the optimal bet size based on the expected return and risk of ruin. It aims to maximize the growth rate of the trader's account while minimizing the probability of large losses.

- **Example:** A trader with a winning probability of 60% and a risk-reward ratio of 2:1 would use the Kelly Criterion formula to calculate the optimal position size: Kelly% = (Winning Probability x (Reward-Risk Ratio + 1) - 1) / (Reward-Risk Ratio) = (0.6 x (2+1) - 1) / 2 = 0.1, or 10% of the account balance.

Volatility-Based Position Sizing

- **Description:** The Volatility-Based Position Sizing method adjusts the position size based on the historical volatility of the asset. This approach takes into account market conditions, allowing traders to allocate more capital to less volatile assets and less capital to more volatile assets.

- **Example:** A trader using the Average True Range (ATR) indicator may decide to risk 1% of their account equity per trade and adjust the position size based on the ATR value. If the ATR value is high, the trader would use a smaller position size, while a lower ATR value would result in a larger position size.

Optimal f

- **Description:** The Optimal f method is used to determine the position size that maximises the geometric growth rate of a trader's account. This approach focuses on maximising long-term growth while considering the risk of ruin.

- **Example:** A trader backtests their trading system and finds that the optimal f value is 0.25. This means that the trader should risk 25% of their account equity on each trade to maximise the geometric growth rate. However, it's essential to note that using the optimal f value in practice might be too aggressive for most traders, as it can lead to significant drawdowns. Therefore, it's often recommended to use a fraction of the optimal f value, such as 50% or 25%, to balance growth and risk.

Monte Carlo Simulation

- **Description:** The Monte Carlo Simulation method uses random sampling and statistical modelling to estimate the optimal position size based on various scenarios and the trader's risk tolerance. This approach provides a more robust estimate of the optimal position size by considering a wide range of market conditions and potential outcomes.

- **Example:** A trader inputs their trading system's historical performance data, desired risk level, and other relevant parameters into a Monte Carlo simulation software. The software generates thousands of possible scenarios and calculates the optimal position size based on the trader's risk tolerance and the probability of achieving the desired trading objectives.

Each position sizing method has its advantages and drawbacks, and the choice of method will depend on the trader's risk tolerance, trading strategy, and personal preferences. By selecting an appropriate position sizing method and consistently applying it, traders can effectively manage their risk, protect their capital, and improve their overall trading performance.

Stop Loss Adjustments

Definition and Explanation

The technique of adjusting stop loss levels in an existing position, known as Stop Loss Adjustment, is employed with the goal of enhancing the risk-reward ratio of the trade. This strategy involves modifying the stop loss levels to improve the overall risk-reward balance of the trade.

The Rationale Behind Adjusting Stop Loss Levels When Adding to a Position

Adjusting stop loss levels when adding to a position can help traders achieve better risk-reward ratios by minimising the potential loss on the initial position while allowing for additional gains on the new trade entry. This strategy can be particularly useful when a trade moves in the intended direction, and the trader wants to capitalise on the momentum without significantly increasing the overall risk.

The Role of Stop Loss Adjustment in Risk Management and Improving Risk-Reward Ratios

Stop loss adjustment plays an essential role in risk management by limiting potential losses on a trade while maintaining exposure to potential profits. By adjusting the stop loss level when adding to a position, traders can effectively reduce the risk on their initial entry while increasing the potential profit on the added position. This approach can lead to more favourable risk-reward ratios, which are crucial for long-term trading success.

Advantages and Disadvantages of Using Stop Loss Adjustment

Advantages

- **Improved risk-reward ratios:** Adjusting stop loss levels when adding to a position can help traders achieve more attractive risk-reward ratios by minimising potential losses and maximising potential profits.

- **Better capital allocation:** Stop loss adjustment allows traders to allocate their capital more efficiently by taking advantage of favourable market conditions without significantly increasing their overall risk.

- **Greater flexibility:** This strategy provides traders with the flexibility to adapt their trade management approach based on the evolving market conditions and the performance of their open positions.

Disadvantages

- **Increased complexity:** Managing multiple stop loss levels and adjusting them when adding to a position can increase the complexity of trade management, potentially leading to confusion and mistakes.

- **Potential for premature exits:** Adjusting stop loss levels too aggressively may lead to premature exits from trades that could have otherwise turned profitable.

- **Market volatility:** In highly volatile markets, adjusting stop loss levels may not always provide the desired risk-reward ratio improvement, as rapid price fluctuations can lead to stop loss orders being triggered unexpectedly.

Best Practices for Implementing Stop Loss Adjustment in Different Market Conditions

- **Assess market conditions:** Before adjusting stop loss levels, traders should carefully analyse the current market conditions and the underlying factors driving price action to determine if the adjustment is warranted.

- **Use technical analysis tools:** Traders can employ various technical analysis tools, such as trend lines, support and resistance levels, and moving averages, to help identify optimal stop loss adjustment levels.

- **Maintain a risk management plan:** It is essential to have a comprehensive risk management plan in place, outlining the maximum acceptable risk per trade and overall portfolio risk, to ensure that stop loss adjustments do not expose the trader to excessive risk.

- **Monitor the trade closely:** After adjusting stop loss levels, traders should closely monitor the trade's progress to determine if further adjustments are needed or if the position should be closed entirely.

- **Stay disciplined:** Traders should maintain discipline in their trade management approach, sticking to their predefined risk management plan and avoiding impulsive decisions driven by fear or greed.

Adapting Trade Management Strategies to Changing Market Conditions

Dynamic trade management involves adapting and adjusting trade management strategies based on changing market conditions. By staying flexible and responsive to market fluctuations, traders can optimise their trade outcomes and better manage risk. This may include adjusting stop loss levels, profit targets, position sizes, or entry and exit criteria based on market volatility, trend strength, or other factors.

Incorporating Technical Analysis and Indicators for Trade Management Updates

Technical analysis and indicators can play a vital role in dynamic trade management by providing actionable information about market conditions, trend strength, and potential reversal points. Some commonly used technical indicators for dynamic trade management include:

- **Moving Averages:** Traders can use moving averages to identify trend direction, support and resistance levels, and potential entry and exit points.

- **Bollinger Bands:** These bands can help traders identify periods of high and low volatility, as well as potential trend reversals.

- **Average True Range (ATR):** ATR is a measure of volatility that can be used to adjust stop loss levels, position size, or profit targets based on market volatility.

- **Relative Strength Index (RSI):** RSI is a momentum indicator that can help traders identify overbought or oversold conditions, as well as potential trend reversals.

The Role of Dynamic Trade Management in Risk Management

Dynamic trade management can play a crucial role in risk management by:

- **Adapting to Changing Market Conditions:** By adjusting trade management strategies based on market conditions, traders can better manage risk and optimise trade outcomes.

- **Limiting Losses:** Dynamic trade management allows traders to adjust stop loss levels, profit targets, or position sizes based on market volatility or trend strength, helping to limit losses and protect profits.

- **Improving Risk-Reward Ratio:** By incorporating technical analysis and indicators into trade management updates, traders can better align their strategies with the potential risk and reward of a trade.

Examples of Dynamic Trade Management Strategies in Different Market Conditions

- **Trend Trading:** In a strong trending market, traders may choose to use a trailing stop to lock in profits as the market moves in their favour. They may also use moving averages or other trend-following indicators to identify potential entry and exit points.

- **Range-Bound Markets:** In a range-bound market, traders may opt for fixed profit targets and stop loss levels, based on support and resistance levels. They may also use oscillators like RSI or Stochastic to identify overbought and oversold conditions for potential reversals.

- **High Volatility Markets:** During periods of high market volatility, traders can adjust their position sizes, stop loss levels, or profit targets based on the increased volatility. Using an indicator like ATR can help traders manage risk in these conditions.

By implementing dynamic trade management strategies that adapt to changing market conditions and incorporate technical analysis and indicators, traders can effectively manage risk, optimise trade outcomes, and improve the overall performance of their trading system.

Chapter - Building and Refining Your System

Building a Comprehensive Trade Management System

Integrating Multiple Trade Management Strategies for a Balanced Approach

A comprehensive trade management system should integrate multiple strategies to create a balanced approach that caters to various market conditions and trading objectives. By combining different techniques such as trailing stops, profit targets, position sizing, and dynamic trade management, traders can optimise their trade outcomes while effectively managing risk. It is essential to select strategies that complement one another and align with the trader's overall trading plan and goals.

Evaluating Trade Management Performance and Making Adjustments

To ensure the effectiveness of a trade management system, traders should continuously evaluate its performance and make adjustments as needed. This can involve:

- **Analysing trade outcomes:** Review individual trades and overall portfolio performance to identify strengths and weaknesses in the trade management system.

- **Backtesting:** Test the trade management strategies on historical market data to assess their effectiveness and identify potential improvements.

- **Forward testing:** Apply the trade management strategies in a simulated or live trading environment to confirm their real-world effectiveness.

- **Making adjustments:** Fine-tune the trade management strategies based on the results of the evaluation, focusing on improving risk management, trade outcomes, and consistency.

The Role of a Comprehensive Trade Management System in Risk Management

A well-designed trade management system plays a crucial role in risk management by:

- **Limiting losses:** Effective trade management strategies can help limit losses by controlling the impact of individual trades on the overall account balance.

- **Balancing risk and reward:** A comprehensive trade management system should strive to achieve a favourable risk-reward ratio by aligning trade sizes, stop loss levels, and profit targets with market conditions and the trader's objectives.

- **Enhancing consistency:** By incorporating multiple trade management strategies, a comprehensive system can improve consistency in trade outcomes, leading to more predictable and stable trading performance.

Best Practices for Developing and Maintaining a Successful Trade Management System

- Align the trade management system with your trading strategy, risk tolerance, and objectives.

- Integrate multiple trade management strategies to create a balanced approach that adapts to various market conditions.

- Regularly evaluate the performance of your trade management system and make adjustments as needed to optimise trade outcomes and risk management.

- Stay disciplined and consistently apply your trade management strategies to ensure long-term success.

- Continuously learn and improve your trade management system by staying informed about new strategies, tools, and market developments.

By developing and maintaining a comprehensive trade management system, traders can effectively manage risk, optimise trade outcomes, and achieve consistent trading performance. This, in turn, will contribute to the overall success of their trading endeavours.

Trade monitoring is a crucial aspect of successful trading, as it enables traders to track their positions, stay updated on market developments, and make informed decisions in real-time.

In this section of the course, we'll delve into the following key components of trade monitoring:

Real-time Chart Analysis

- **Technical Analysis:** We'll explore various charting techniques, patterns, and indicators that traders can use to analyse price action and identify potential trading opportunities. These tools include support and resistance levels, moving averages, trendlines, and oscillators, among others.

- **Fundamental Analysis:** This component will cover the importance of understanding economic data releases, earnings reports, and other macroeconomic factors that can impact the markets. We'll discuss how to interpret these events and integrate them into your trading decisions.

Staying Updated with News and Events

Understanding how news and events can influence the markets is essential for trade monitoring. We'll discuss the significance of staying informed about market-moving events, such as central bank announcements, geopolitical developments, and major economic indicators. You'll learn strategies for staying up-to-date with these events and how to react to unexpected news.

Types of News and Events

Central Bank Announcements

Central banks are vital institutions that play a critical role in shaping economic policy and influencing financial markets. Their actions and announcements can have significant effects on currency, bond, and equity markets. In this section, we'll delve into the different types of central bank announcements and how to monitor and interpret them to make informed trading decisions.

Types of Central Bank Announcements

- **Interest Rate Decisions:** Central banks set interest rates to control inflation, stabilise the economy, and maintain currency strength. Interest rate decisions can greatly impact the financial markets, as they affect borrowing costs, investment returns, and currency valuations. Traders should pay close attention to these decisions and the accompanying statements, as they can offer insights into the central bank's outlook on the economy.

- **Monetary Policy Updates:** Central banks periodically release statements and updates on their monetary policy, which can include details on quantitative easing (QE) programs, asset purchases, or other policy tools. These updates can provide valuable information on the central bank's assessment of the economy and its intentions for future policy actions, which can influence market sentiment and trading opportunities.

- **Inflation Reports:** Central banks monitor inflation closely, as it is a key indicator of economic stability. Inflation reports typically contain data on consumer prices, producer prices, and other inflation metrics, as well as the central bank's analysis of the inflationary environment. Traders can use this information to anticipate potential changes in monetary policy and gauge the central bank's stance on future interest rate decisions.

Monitoring Central Bank Announcements

- **Central Bank Websites:** One of the most reliable sources for central bank announcements is the central banks' own websites. These sites typically have a dedicated section for press releases, policy statements, and other relevant information. Make sure to check these websites regularly to stay informed about upcoming announcements and updates.

- **Financial News Outlets:** Major financial news outlets, such as Bloomberg, Reuters, and CNBC, often provide real-time coverage of central bank announcements, along with expert analysis and commentary. By following these sources, traders can quickly access the latest information and understand its implications for the financial markets.

- **Economic Calendars:** Economic calendars are essential tools for keeping track of scheduled central bank announcements and other market-moving events. These calendars typically list the dates and times of upcoming events, along with their expected impact on the markets. By using an economic calendar, traders can prepare for central bank announcements and adjust their trading strategies accordingly.

Interpreting Central Bank Announcements

Understanding the Central Bank's Stance: When interpreting central bank announcements, it is crucial to grasp the central bank's stance on economic conditions, inflation, and growth prospects. This information can help traders anticipate potential policy changes and understand how these changes may influence the markets.

- **Analysing Market Reaction:** Central bank announcements can trigger significant market volatility, especially if they contain unexpected information or policy shifts. Traders should closely monitor market reactions to these announcements, as they can provide valuable insights into market sentiment and potential trading opportunities.

- **Adjusting Trading Strategies:** Based on the analysis of central bank announcements and their implications for the markets, traders may need to adjust their trading strategies accordingly. This can include modifying stop-loss orders, reevaluating profit targets, or adjusting position sizes to account for increased volatility or changing market conditions.

Interpreting central bank announcements, traders can stay informed about crucial economic policy decisions and their potential impact on the financial markets. This knowledge can help traders make better-informed trading decisions and more effectively manage their risk in the face of market-moving events.

Geopolitical Developments

Geopolitical developments, including political elections, international conflicts, and trade disputes, can have significant effects on financial markets. These events can lead to shifts in investor sentiment and changes in economic policy, both of which can create new trading opportunities or pose risks to existing positions. In this section, we'll examine various types of geopolitical developments and discuss strategies for staying informed about these events and assessing their potential impacts on your trading strategy.

Types of Geopolitical Developments

- **Political Elections:** Elections can have a significant impact on a country's economic policy and investment climate. The outcome of an election can lead to policy changes that affect taxation, government spending, and regulations, which in turn can influence financial markets. Traders should be aware of upcoming elections in the countries where they trade and be prepared to adjust their strategies based on potential policy shifts.

- **International Conflicts:** Conflicts between countries, such as wars, territorial disputes, and diplomatic tensions, can create uncertainty in financial markets and affect the valuation of assets. These conflicts can lead to changes in commodity prices, currency values, and stock market performance, making it crucial for traders to monitor ongoing international conflicts and assess their potential impact on their trading strategies.

- **Trade Disputes:** Trade disputes, such as tariffs, import/export restrictions, and sanctions, can disrupt international trade and affect the economies of the countries involved. These disputes can have wide-ranging effects on currency values, stock markets, and commodity prices, which can create new trading opportunities or pose risks to existing positions.

Staying Informed About Geopolitical Developments

- **News Outlets:** Major news outlets, such as BBC, CNN, and Al Jazeera, provide up-to-date information on geopolitical developments around the world. By following these sources, traders can stay informed about ongoing events and their potential impact on financial markets.

- **Government and International Organization Websites:** Official websites of governments and international organisations, such as the United Nations or the World Trade Organization, can provide reliable information on geopolitical events and policy changes. These sources can help traders gain a deeper understanding of the context and implications of various developments.

- **Social Media:** Social media platforms, such as Twitter and Facebook, can be valuable sources of real-time information on geopolitical events. By following influential figures, news organisations, and experts in the field, traders can receive timely updates and insights on important events as they unfold.

Assessing the Impact of Geopolitical Developments on Trading Strategies

- **Analysing Market Reactions:** When a geopolitical event occurs, it is essential to observe the market's reaction to understand its potential impact on your trading strategy. This analysis can help traders identify new opportunities or risks and make necessary adjustments to their positions.

- **Evaluating Potential Policy Changes:** Geopolitical developments can lead to policy changes that affect the economic environment and financial markets. Traders should assess the likelihood of these changes and consider their potential impact on their trading strategies.

- **Incorporating Geopolitical Risk into Trading Decisions:** By staying informed about geopolitical developments and understanding their potential effects on the markets, traders can incorporate geopolitical risk into their trading decisions. This can involve adjusting position sizes, stop-loss orders, and profit targets to account for increased market volatility or uncertainty.

By monitoring geopolitical developments and understanding their potential impact on financial markets, traders can more effectively manage their risk and capitalise on new opportunities. Staying informed about these events and assessing their potential effects on your trading strategy is crucial for navigating the ever-changing global economy.

Economic Indicators

Economic indicators are essential tools for traders, as they provide valuable insights into the health of an economy and its future prospects. These indicators can affect market trends and influence trading opportunities. In this section, we'll examine the most important economic indicators, how they can impact financial markets, and how to incorporate them into your trading analysis.

Types of Economic Indicators

- **Gross Domestic Product (GDP):** GDP is the total value of goods and services produced within a country over a specific period. It is considered the broadest measure of economic activity and serves as an indicator of a country's economic health. Changes in GDP can influence currency values, stock markets, and interest rates.

- **Employment Figures:** Employment data, such as the unemployment rate and non-farm payrolls, offer insights into the labour market's strength. Strong employment figures can signal a healthy economy, while rising unemployment can indicate economic weakness. Employment data can impact currency values, as well as consumer spending and overall economic growth.

- **Inflation:** Inflation measures the rate at which the general level of prices for goods and services is rising, eroding the purchasing power of money. Central banks often target specific inflation rates to maintain price stability, and changes in inflation can influence interest rate decisions, currency values, and bond markets.

- **Consumer Sentiment:** Consumer sentiment indicators, such as the Consumer Confidence Index, gauge how optimistic consumers are about the economy's future. High consumer confidence can lead to increased spending and economic growth, while low confidence can result in reduced spending and economic stagnation. Consumer sentiment can impact stock markets, currency values, and consumer-related sectors of the   economy.

- **Manufacturing and Services Data:** Indicators like the Purchasing Managers' Index (PMI) provide insights into the health of the manufacturing and services sectors. These indices can signal expansion or contraction in these sectors, which can impact stock markets, currency values, and overall economic growth.

Monitoring Economic Indicators

- **Economic Calendars:** Traders can use economic calendars to stay informed about upcoming economic data releases. These calendars typically include the date, time, and importance of each release, as well as the market's consensus expectations.

- **News Outlets and Financial Websites:** Major news outlets and financial websites, such as Bloomberg, Reuters, and CNBC, provide regular updates on economic indicator releases and expert analysis of their implications.

- **Government and Central Bank Websites:** Official websites of governments and central banks can provide the most accurate and up-to-date information on economic indicators, as well as additional context and analysis.

Incorporating Economic Indicators into Trading Analysis

- **Identifying Market Reactions:** When economic data is released, traders should observe the market's reaction to gauge its potential impact on their trading strategies. Significant deviations from market expectations can cause increased volatility and create new trading opportunities.

- **Assessing the Broader Economic Environment:** Understanding the current state of the economy and its potential trajectory can help traders identify trends and make more informed trading decisions. By regularly monitoring economic indicators, traders can gain insights into the overall economic environment and adjust their strategies accordingly.
- **Adjusting Trading Strategies Based on Economic Indicators:** Traders can use economic indicators to fine-tune their trading strategies, adjusting position sizes, stop-loss orders, and profit targets based on the current economic environment and market conditions.

By closely monitoring economic indicators and understanding their potential impact on financial markets, traders can more effectively manage their risk and capitalise on new opportunities. Incorporating these indicators into your trading analysis can provide a solid foundation for making informed decisions.

Staying Informed: News Sources and Platforms - Financial News Websites

In today's fast-paced financial markets, staying informed about market-moving events is crucial for successful trading. Financial news websites are valuable resources that provide up-to-date information on market developments and can help you identify potential trading opportunities. In this section, we'll explore various financial news websites, such as Bloomberg, Reuters, and CNBC, and discuss how to navigate these sites to find relevant news for your trading strategy.

Key Financial News Websites

- **Bloomberg:** Bloomberg is a global leader in financial news, providing comprehensive coverage of market data, company news, and economic indicators. Its website offers live market updates, expert analysis, and in-depth articles on a wide range of topics, making it an essential resource for traders seeking the latest market information.
- **Reuters:** As one of the world's largest international news organisations, Reuters offers extensive coverage of financial markets, including real-time news, market data, and expert analysis. Its financial news platform provides updates on currency, equity, and commodity markets, as well as insights into economic trends and policy developments.
- **CNBC:** CNBC is a leading business and financial news network, offering live market updates, breaking news, and expert analysis. Its website features articles and videos on a variety of financial topics, including stock market news, economic data releases, and company earnings reports.

Navigating Financial News Websites

- **Market Updates:** Most financial news websites feature a live market update section, providing real-time information on market movements, economic data releases, and breaking news. Traders can use these updates to stay informed about market conditions and identify potential trading opportunities.

- **News Categories:** Financial news websites typically organise their content into categories, such as equities, currencies, commodities, and bonds. By focusing on the categories relevant to your trading strategy, you can efficiently find the news that impacts your trades.

- **Customised News Feeds:** Many financial news websites allow users to customise their news feeds by selecting specific markets, asset classes, or topics of interest. By tailoring your news feed to your trading strategy, you can quickly access the information most relevant to your trading decisions.

- **Expert Analysis:** Financial news websites often feature expert analysis and commentary, providing valuable insights into market trends, economic developments, and trading strategies. By following these expert opinions, traders can enhance their understanding of the markets and improve their trading decisions.

Identifying Potential Trading Opportunities

Market Reactions to News: As news breaks, markets can react with increased volatility, creating potential trading opportunities. By monitoring financial news websites for significant market-moving events, traders can quickly capitalise on these opportunities.

- **Earnings Reports:** Company earnings reports can have a significant impact on stock prices, offering potential trading opportunities for equity traders. Financial news websites often provide coverage of earnings releases, including analysis and market reactions.

- **Economic Data Releases:** Major economic data releases, such as employment figures and GDP growth, can impact financial markets and create trading opportunities. By staying informed about these releases through financial news websites, traders can anticipate market reactions and plan their trades accordingly.

By staying informed about market-moving events through financial news websites, traders can better understand the factors influencing financial markets and identify potential trading opportunities. By learning to navigate these websites and customising your news feed to your trading strategy, you can efficiently access the information you need.

Economic Calendars

Economic calendars are essential tools for traders, providing a schedule of upcoming economic events and data releases that can have a significant impact on the financial markets. Staying informed about these events allows traders to prepare for market-moving developments and adjust their trading strategies accordingly. In this section, we'll discuss how to use economic calendars effectively and incorporate them into your trading routine.

Understanding Economic Calendars

- **Components of Economic Calendars:** Economic calendars typically provide information on the date and time of each event, the country or region involved, the event's nature, the previous data release, market expectations, and the actual data once released. This information allows traders to anticipate market reactions and plan their trades around significant events.

- **Importance of Economic Indicators:** Economic indicators, such as GDP, employment figures, and consumer sentiment, provide insights into the health of an economy and can influence market trends. By monitoring these indicators through economic calendars, traders can stay informed about market-moving events and identify potential trading opportunities.

- **Market Impact:** Economic calendars often include a market impact rating, which estimates the potential impact of an event on the financial markets. Events with a higher impact rating are more likely to cause significant market volatility and create trading opportunities.

Using Economic Calendars in Your Trading Strategy

- **Anticipating Market Reactions:** By monitoring economic calendars for upcoming events, traders can anticipate potential market reactions and adjust their trading strategies accordingly. For example, if a major central bank announcement is scheduled, a trader may choose to close or reduce their positions to minimise risk ahead of the event.

- **Planning Trades:** Economic calendars can help traders plan their trades by providing information on the timing and potential impact of market-moving events. By understanding when significant events are scheduled, traders can better manage their trades and capitalise on potential market volatility.

- **Adjusting Stop Losses and Profit Targets:** In anticipation of market-moving events, traders may choose to adjust their stop losses and profit targets to account for increased market volatility. By doing so, they can protect their positions and lock in profits during periods of heightened market uncertainty.

- **Incorporating News Events into Technical Analysis:** Traders can use economic calendars to incorporate news events into their technical analysis. For instance, a trader might monitor support and resistance levels around significant economic data releases, as these levels may be tested or broken due to market reactions to the news.

Traders should observe market reactions, planning trades around significant events, and incorporating news events into technical analysis, traders can capitalise on potential trading opportunities and better manage their risk.

Social Media

In today's fast-paced trading environment, social media platforms such as Twitter and LinkedIn have become indispensable sources of real-time news and market commentary. Staying informed about market-moving events and identifying potential trading opportunities through social media is an essential skill for modern traders. In this section, we'll discuss strategies for leveraging social media to stay informed and identify potential trading opportunities.

Importance of Social Media in Trading

- **Real-time Information:** Social media platforms provide real-time access to news, market commentary, and insights from industry experts. This constant flow of information can help traders stay up-to-date with the latest developments and react quickly to market-moving events.

- **Market Sentiment:** Social media can offer valuable insights into market sentiment, as traders and investors share their opinions and analysis on various financial instruments. By monitoring social media, traders can gauge the overall market sentiment and identify potential trends or reversals.

- **Networking and Learning:** Social media platforms provide opportunities for traders to connect with other professionals, learn from their experiences, and share their own insights. This networking can help traders improve their skills and stay informed about the latest strategies and techniques.

Leveraging Social Media in Trading

- **Following Industry Experts and Influencers:** Traders can benefit from following industry experts, influencers, and financial news outlets on social media platforms. These sources often share valuable market insights, analysis, and news that can help traders make informed decisions.

- **Monitoring Hashtags and Keywords:** By monitoring relevant hashtags and keywords, traders can stay informed about specific financial instruments, market developments, and news events. This can help traders identify potential trading opportunities and stay ahead of the competition.

- **Setting Up Alerts:** Many social media platforms allow users to set up alerts for specific keywords or accounts. By setting up alerts, traders can ensure that they don't miss critical market updates or insights from their favourite sources.

- **Engaging with the Trading Community:** Active participation in the trading community on social media can help traders learn from others, share their own insights, and stay informed about the latest trends and strategies. By engaging with other traders, professionals can expand their knowledge and improve their trading skills.

- **Managing Information Overload:** While social media can provide valuable information, it can also be overwhelming. Traders should develop strategies for managing information overload, such as setting aside dedicated time for social media, using filters and lists to organise content, and focusing on the most relevant sources.

Industry experts, monitoring hashtags and keywords, and engaging with the trading community, traders can capitalise on the wealth of information available on social media platforms and improve their trading skills.

Newsletters and Subscriptions

Subscribing to industry newsletters and financial market analysis can provide valuable insights and help you stay up-to-date with market developments. Keeping informed about the latest news and trends is crucial for making well-informed trading decisions. In this section, we'll explore various subscription options and discuss how to select the most relevant content for your trading needs.

Benefits of Newsletters and Subscriptions

- **Regular Updates:** Newsletters and subscriptions provide regular updates on market developments, helping traders stay informed about the latest news, trends, and analysis. This can help traders make better decisions and adjust their trading strategies accordingly.

- **Expert Insights:** Many newsletters and subscriptions are authored by industry experts and professional traders, offering valuable insights and perspectives on market events. By following these experts, traders can learn from their experience and improve their own trading skills.

- **Tailored Content:** Newsletters and subscriptions often focus on specific financial instruments, markets, or trading strategies, allowing traders to tailor their information sources to their individual needs and interests. This can help traders focus on the most relevant information for their trading goals.

Selecting Newsletters and Subscriptions

- **Assessing Your Needs:** To choose the right newsletters and subscriptions, traders should first assess their specific needs and interests. Consider factors such as the markets you trade, the instruments you focus on, and the type of analysis you prefer.

- **Researching Options:** Once you have a clear understanding of your needs, research various newsletters and subscriptions to find those that align with your interests. Look for reputable sources with a history of providing valuable content and insights.

- **Evaluating Content Quality:** Before subscribing to a newsletter or analysis service, evaluate the quality of their content. Look for well-researched, data-driven insights that can help you make informed trading decisions.

- **Considering Cost:** Many newsletters and subscriptions come with a cost. While some may be worth the investment, it's important to weigh the benefits against the expense. Consider factors such as the quality of the content, the frequency of updates, and the insights provided.

- **Monitoring Performance:** Once you've subscribed to a newsletter or analysis service, monitor the performance of the information provided. If the content is consistently helpful and insightful, it may be worth maintaining the subscription. If not, consider exploring other options.

Newsletters and subscriptions that align with your trading interests will help you stay informed about market developments, gain valuable insights from industry experts, and improve your trading skills. Be sure to evaluate the quality of the content and consider the costs before committing to any subscription services.

Interpreting News and Events

- **Understanding Market Sentiment:** We'll discuss the importance of gauging market sentiment and the role it plays in shaping market trends. You'll learn how to interpret news and events to determine whether they are likely to have a positive or negative impact on the markets.

- **Assessing the Potential Impact of News:** Not all news events will have a significant impact on the markets. We'll discuss how to assess the potential impact of various news events, taking into account factors such as market liquidity, the size of the affected market, and the historical reaction to similar events.

- **Factoring News and Events into Your Trading Strategy:** We'll explore strategies for incorporating news and events into your trading analysis, such as adjusting position sizes, setting stop-loss orders, and modifying profit targets. You'll learn how to react to unexpected news in real-time and make informed decisions based on the potential impact on your trades.

Managing Risk in the Face of News and Events

- **Preparing for Scheduled Events:** We'll discuss strategies for managing risk in the face of scheduled events, such as setting stop-loss orders, adjusting position sizes, and employing contingency plans.

- **Reacting to Unexpected News:** Unexpected news events can cause significant market volatility and pose risks to your trading positions. We'll explore strategies for managing risk in the face of unexpected news

Development of a Trading System

The development of a well-structured trading system is crucial for success in financial markets. A robust trading system provides a disciplined, systematic approach to trading, helping to remove emotional biases and impulsive actions that can result in significant losses. It outlines your entry and exit strategies, risk and money management protocols, and other key components that offer a roadmap for navigating the markets. By having a concrete set of rules to follow, traders can evaluate their performance, refine their tactics, and enhance their ability to capitalise on market opportunities.

In the following sections, we will work through an example of developing a trading system based on using multiple timeframes to confirm the market trend. The aim is to help you work through the thought process of developing the essential elements of a successful trading system. Throughout the process of developing this system, I will ask a number of questions. These are the types of questions you should be asking yourself when you are developing a new trading system.

Multi-timeframe analysis can be an excellent way to get a more nuanced understanding of the market's direction, sentiment, and potential turning points. Here's a trading strategy based on this approach:

Multi-Timeframe Moving Average Trend Confirmation
Markets: Stocks, Forex, Commodities, Cryptocurrencies

Idea
The core concept is to use two or more different timeframes to confirm the trend direction before entering a trade. This helps filter out false signals that could appear when looking at just a single timeframe.

Components

Longer Timeframe (e.g., Daily Chart): Utilise a long-term moving average (e.g., 200-day MA) to identify the primary trend.

- Trend is up when the price is above the 200-day MA.
- Trend is down when the price is below the 200-day MA.

Shorter Timeframe (e.g., 1-hour or 4-hour Chart): Use a shorter moving average (e.g., 50-period MA) to time your entry and exit.

- Buy when the price crosses above the 50-period MA and the longer timeframe confirms an upward trend.
- Sell when the price crosses below the 50-period MA and the longer timeframe confirms a downward trend.

Risk Management
- Use stop-loss orders based on volatility or a fixed percentage from entry.
- Make sure to adhere to your capital allocation rules, adjusting for the lower frequency but higher reliability of signals from the multi-timeframe analysis.

Strengths
- Reduced false signals due to multi-timeframe confirmation.
- Can be applied across different markets.

Weaknesses
- Requires discipline in keeping up with multiple timeframes.
- Potentially lower trade frequency, depending on the timeframes chosen.

Example: Step by Step Development of a Trading System

Now that we have an overall concept for our trading system, lets look step-by-step on how we might develop this multi-timeframe moving average trend confirmation system.

Step 1: Understanding the Objective

- **Objective:** The aim of this strategy is to capture significant trends in the market while minimising false signals. This is achieved by using two different timeframes to confirm the trend direction before making a trade.

Do you understand what a trend is in trading, and why it's crucial to identify it correctly?

Step 2: Choosing the Markets

Markets to Trade: You can apply this strategy across different markets such as stocks, forex, commodities, or cryptocurrencies. Since you're starting out, let's stick to just one or two markets to keep things simple.

Have you decided which market you're interested in trading?

Step 3: Setting Up the Charts

Longer Timeframe: Choose a longer timeframe like the Daily chart and apply a 200-day Moving Average (MA).

Shorter Timeframe: Opt for a shorter timeframe like the 1-hour or 4-hour chart and add a 50-period MA.

Do you know how to set up moving averages on a trading chart?

Step 4: Identifying the Trend

Primary Trend on Longer Timeframe

- Trend is up when the price is above the 200-day MA.
- Trend is down when the price is below the 200-day MA.

Entry Criteria on Shorter Timeframe:

- Buy when the price crosses above the 50-period MA, and the longer timeframe confirms an upward trend.
- Sell when the price crosses below the 50-period MA, and the longer timeframe confirms a downward trend.

Does the idea of trend confirmation between two timeframes make sense to you?

Step 5: Risk Management

Risk per Trade: Let's start conservatively by risking no more than 1% of your trading capital on a single trade.

Stop-Loss: Place a stop-loss to limit your losses. A good rule of thumb is to set it at 2-3% below (for a buy order) or above (for a sell order) your entry price.

Are you familiar with the concept of risk management, particularly stop-losses?

Step 6: Backtest and Paper Trade

Before putting real money on the line, it's vital to backtest your strategy on historical data.

You can also practise by paper trading in real time.

Have you ever backtested a trading strategy before?

Review - How does our system fit the initial objective ?

Objective: The aim of this strategy is to capture significant trends in the market while minimising false signals.

Understanding why a system is built a certain way is crucial for grasping its strengths and weaknesses.

Let's explore how the multi-timeframe moving average trend confirmation system aligns with the stated objective.

Objective Alignment

Capturing Significant Trends

Longer Timeframe (200-day MA): The 200-day moving average on the daily chart helps to identify the primary trend, which is likely to be a significant one given the extended timeframe. Long trends mean more significant potential gains.

Shorter Timeframe (50-period MA): Once the longer-term trend is identified, the shorter timeframe is used for entering the trade at a more optimal point, allowing you to ride the primary trend with better timing.

Do you see how using a longer timeframe aids in capturing the significant, lasting trends in the market?

Minimising False Signals

Two Timeframe Confirmation: By requiring the trend to be confirmed on both a long and short timeframe, the system filters out many false signals that might occur on just one timeframe. For instance, a price spike on the shorter timeframe may not affect the longer-term trend.

Stop-Loss Management: By implementing a strict stop-loss, you minimise the impact of those signals that do turn out to be false. Remember, the aim isn't to eliminate all false signals but to minimise their impact.

Does the idea of using two timeframes make sense as a way to filter out false or misleading signals?

This alignment between system design and objective is a cornerstone of successful trading strategy development. It helps not just in executing the trades but also in maintaining the discipline to stick to the system, especially when it hits a rough patch, as all systems do. Are you clear on how this system fits with its trading objectives?

Risk / Stop Loss Management

Sop-loss management is pivotal in any trading system, especially in a multi-timeframe approach that aims to capture long-term trends while minimising false signals. Here's a walk-through of some popular stop-loss strategies that can be integrated into our multi-timeframe system:

Fixed Stop-Loss

How it Works: You set a fixed distance from your entry point where the stop-loss will be placed. This is the simplest type of stop-loss and is measured in pips, points, or a percentage from the entry price.

Pros & Cons: Easy to implement but can often get triggered by market 'noise' rather than a meaningful change in trend.

Do you see the pros and cons of a fixed stop-loss?

Trailing Stop-Loss

How it Works: As the trade moves in your favour, the stop-loss is moved (or 'trailed') to lock in gains. This can either be done manually or automatically.

Pros & Cons: Allows gains to run while protecting against reversals. However, setting it too tight can get you stopped out prematurely.

How do you feel about a trailing stop-loss?

ATR-Based Stop-Loss

How it Works: The Average True Range (ATR) indicator measures market volatility. The stop-loss is set as a multiple of ATR away from the entry price.

Pros & Cons: Adapts to market conditions but might have you exiting too soon in a highly volatile market.

Would the adaptive nature of ATR-based stops appeal to you?

Time-Based Stop-Loss

How it Works: If the trade doesn't move in your favour within a set period, the stop-loss is triggered.

Pros & Cons: Good for strategies with a specific expected timeframe. Not suitable for strategies looking to capture long-term trends.

Break-Even Stop

How it Works: Once the trade moves a predetermined distance in your favour, the stop-loss is moved to the entry point. This ensures that, from that moment on, the worst-case scenario is that the trade closes at break-even, not at a loss.

Pros & Cons: Locks in a risk-free trade after a certain point, allowing some peace of mind. However, if set too early, market volatility can trigger the stop and exit the trade before the real trend move occurs.

Would you like to include this as a fixed rule, or would you make it adaptable based on the performance of the trade or current market conditions?

Combined Strategies

How it Works: Use a combination of the above strategies. For example, you could start with an ATR-based stop-loss and then switch to a trailing stop once the trade moves in your favour.

Pros & Cons: Customizable and adaptable but can be complicated to implement and may require regular adjustments.

Would you consider a combined approach for more nuance?

Understanding the pros and cons of each stop-loss strategy will help you select the most appropriate one for the trading system we're developing. It's a good idea to backtest different stop-loss strategies to see which works best in historical scenarios. Would you like to dive deeper into backtesting these stop-loss strategies?

Profit Targets

Adding profit targets can be a valuable aspect of your trading strategy. They can help ensure that you capture profits in a systematic way rather than relying solely on market behaviour.

Let's discuss a few different types of profit targets:

Fixed Profit Target

How it Works: As soon as you enter a trade, set a predefined price level for taking profit.

Pros & Cons: Simple to implement and ensures that you take profit at a level you're comfortable with. However, it can sometimes limit your profits if the asset keeps moving in a favourable direction after you've exited.

Trailing Stop Profit

How it Works: This is similar to a stop-loss but in the opposite direction. As the price moves in your favour, the "trailing stop" moves with it. When the price reverses by a predefined amount, the system exits the trade.

Pros & Cons: Allows for more flexibility and can capture larger profits during strong trends. The downside is that market noise can sometimes trigger an exit, leading to smaller profits.

Time-Based Exit

How it Works: Exit the trade after a fixed amount of time has elapsed, regardless of profit or loss.

Pros & Cons: Can prevent you from holding onto losing trades for too long but may also exit profitable trades prematurely.

Fibonacci or Percentage Retracements

How it Works: Use Fibonacci levels or a set percentage as your profit target.

Pros & Cons: The market often respects these levels, making them reliable targets. However, they are more complex to implement.

Multiple Targets (Scaling Out)

How it Works: Instead of setting one profit target, you can set multiple and scale out of your position as each target is hit.

Pros & Cons: This method allows you to capture profits while still leaving some room for the trade to run further in your favour. The downside is that it complicates trade management.
Which of these profit target strategies do you think would best complement our multi-timeframe trading system? Would you consider using a combination of these methods?

Adding to an existing Position / Pyramiding

Pyramiding involves adding to a winning position to take fuller advantage of a market trend.

Basic Pyramiding Strategy

- **Initial Position:** Start with a basic trade unit — say, 100 shares of a stock or 1 contract in futures.

- **First Profit Target Hit:** When the trade moves in your favour and hits your first profit target, you add another unit to your position typically on a pullback.

- **Subsequent Levels:** Continue this process, adding more to your position as the market moves in your favour, hitting predetermined levels.

Pros: Can greatly amplify your profits in a strong trend.

Cons: Adds complexity and can amplify losses if the trend reverses and you haven't set appropriate stop losses.

Key Considerations

Risk Management: It's crucial to adjust your stop losses as you add to the position.

Entry Points: Decide in advance where you'll add to your positions. These should be logical levels based on technical analysis.

Maximum Size: Have a predefined maximum size to prevent overexposure.

When implementing a pyramiding strategy, would you prefer to pyramid aggressively, adding large units, or more conservatively, adding smaller units as the trade progresses in your favour?

Lets say for this example we wish to adding medium to smaller units as the trade progresses, ideally looking to do this on a retracement, perhaps on a 50% or 60.8% retracement Fibonacci level

Steps for Implementing Your Strategy

- **Initial Position:** Take your initial position based on your multi-timeframe analysis.

- **Adjust Stop-Loss:** Set your initial stop-loss. As the trade moves in your favour, use a trailing stop or adjust your stop-loss manually to lock in gains.

- **First Profit Target:** Identify your first profit target. Once it's reached, consider adding to your position on a retracement.

- **Fibonacci Retracement Levels:** Look for the price to pull back to a 50% or 61.8% Fibonacci retracement level. When it does, and if the higher timeframe trend is still intact, add a medium or smaller unit to your position.

- **Review Stop-Loss:** Each time you add to the position, review and possibly adjust your stop-loss to manage your risk effectively.

- **Subsequent Levels:** Continue to pyramid your position, always mindful of your predetermined maximum position size.

- **Break-Even Stop:** Once the trade has moved sufficiently in your favour, adjust your stop-loss to the break-even point.

Risk Management

Predefined Levels: Have a predefined maximum number of units that you'll hold, to avoid overexposing yourself.

Continuous Monitoring: Keep an eye on different timeframes to ensure that the overall trend hasn't changed against you.

Profit Targets

You can also set additional profit targets where you'll either take partial profits or exit the trade entirely.

Does this sort of pyramiding strategy align with your trading philosophy and risk tolerance?

Would you like to explore additional exit strategies such as using trailing stops or price targets based on Fibonacci extensions?

Fine-tuning your exit strategies can make a significant difference in your trading performance.

Let's explore two key approaches: Trailing Stops and Fibonacci Extensions.

Trailing Stops

Fixed Trailing Stop: You set a fixed distance from the market price. For instance, if your stock is trading at $50, you could set a trailing stop at $45. As the stock rises, the stop adjusts itself. If the stock falls, the stop remains fixed.

Dynamic Trailing Stop: This type uses a percentage instead of a fixed number. For example, a 5% dynamic trailing stop on a $100 stock sets the sell stop at $95. If the stock rises to $110, the new selling price would adjust to $104.5.

Volatility-Based Trailing Stop: Some traders use indicators like Average True Range (ATR) to set a trailing stop based on market volatility.

Time-Based Trailing Stop: For example, you could tighten your trailing stop if a trade has been open for a certain number of days or after certain market events.

Fibonacci Extensions

Initial Extension: A common initial target could be the 138.2% or 161.8% Fibonacci extension of the last major move. These levels can act as profit targets where you either scale out of the position or close it entirely.

Subsequent Levels: Further extensions like 200% or 261.8% can act as secondary targets for longer-term trades.

Scaling Out: As with your entry strategy, you could use these extensions to scale out of a position progressively. For instance, selling half your position at the 138.2% level, and the rest at the 200% level.

Combining Strategies

You could combine these strategies for more nuanced trade management. For example, you might use a trailing stop to protect against downside risk while setting profit targets at Fibonacci extension levels to capture upside potential.

Let's consider hypothetical scenarios for a deeper understanding. Since we're simulating, please remember that these examples are illustrative and not indicative of actual trading outcomes.

Scenario 1: Bullish Market

Fixed Trailing Stop: You enter at $100 with a $5 trailing stop. The stock rises to $150. Your stop would have moved to $145. A subsequent drop to $144 triggers the stop. You exit at $145, capturing a $45 gain per share.

Dynamic Trailing Stop (5%): You enter at $100, setting a 5% stop at $95. Stock moves to $150. Your stop adjusts to $142.5. A drop to $142 triggers the stop. You make a $42 gain per share.

Fibonacci Extensions: You target 161.8% extension which gives you an exit price of $161.8. You exit when the price hits this level, capturing a $61.8 gain per share.

Scenario 2: Sideways Market

Fixed Trailing Stop: The stock oscillates between $100 and $110. Your $5 trailing stop could be hit during these oscillations, exiting you at a slight profit or even a loss.

Dynamic Trailing Stop (5%): Same as fixed, but a little more adaptive. It can potentially keep you in the trade longer, but in a choppy market, you might still get stopped out prematurely.

Fibonacci Extensions: Since you've set high extension levels, you're still holding your position, waiting for a breakout.

Scenario 3: Bearish Market

Fixed Trailing Stop: You enter at $100 with a $5 stop. The stock falls to $90. Your stop at $95 triggers, and you take a $5 loss per share.

Dynamic Trailing Stop (5%): You enter at $100. Stop is at $95. The stock falls to $90, triggering your stop, similar to the fixed trailing stop.

Fibonacci Extensions: If you're aiming for high extension levels, you wouldn't have a predefined exit in a bearish market and might face higher losses unless you've set a stop loss.

How do you think these exit strategies fit into your trading plan? Would you consider using one over the other based on the market condition?

How would you adjust the trailing stops in your system to allow for normal market fluctuations while still providing downside protection?

Would you consider using volatility measures like the Average True Range (ATR) to set a more adaptive stop?

Both the Average True Range (ATR) and the Donchian Channel methods are well-regarded for setting adaptive stops, and they allow you to adjust the stop size based on the market's own behaviour. Your idea of dynamically setting the Donchian 'X' days parameter based on the current cycle length could add an extra layer of adaptability. The 2/3 ratio you suggested could be a sensible starting point for balancing reactivity and security in your stop setting.

By tying the cycle length to 'X', you would essentially be making the system more adaptive to prevailing market conditions. This means the system would naturally allow for larger fluctuations during more volatile periods and tighten up during quieter times.

What do you think about applying this same concept of dynamic adjustments to other parts of the trading system as well? Would you adjust your entry or profit target strategies dynamically based on prevailing conditions?

Considering dynamic adjustments to various components of your trading system can offer a more nuanced and adaptive approach. For example, if you're using a moving average for entry signals, you could consider employing a dynamic lookback period that adapts to current market volatility, similar to how you adjust the 'X' days in your Donchian Channel-based stop-loss.

For profit targets, some traders use Adaptive Fibonacci Extensions based on prevailing volatility or even trend strength. This could be an effective way to lock in profits during highly favourable conditions, while also allowing room for the trade to run during less decisive periods.

Considering you're aiming for a basket of diverse and low-correlated systems, how do you feel these dynamic adjustments could fit into your overall trading strategy? Would they complement the other strategies you have in place?

Here is the complete trading strategy based on our discussions. This strategy aims to capture significant trends while minimising false signals, using multi-timeframe analysis and robust risk management techniques.

Objective

Capture significant market trends while minimising false signals by employing a multi-timeframe approach for confirmation.

Entry Rules

Long Position

- Primary Timeframe: Price is above the 200-day moving average.
- Secondary Timeframe: Price crosses above the 50-period moving average.

Short Position

- Primary Timeframe: Price is below the 200-day moving average.
- Secondary Timeframe: Price crosses below the 50-period moving average.

Money Management

- Risk no more than 1% of total capital on a single trade.
- Allocate a larger portion of capital for rare signals.

Risk Management

- Do not have more than 5% of capital at risk at any given time.

Stop Loss Management

- **Initial Stop:** Placed at 2/3rds of the current market cycle, based on a Donchian channel with 'X' days lookback (where X = 2/3rd of the current cycle length).

- **Break-even Stop:** Once the trade moves in favour by a predefined amount ($5 for instance), move the stop loss to break-even.

Profit Targets and Multiple Exits

- **Scaling Out:** Partially close the position at predefined levels to lock in some profits. For instance, close 50% of the position when the trade moves in your favour by $10.

- **Fibonacci Extensions:** Use Fibonacci extension levels such as 138.2%, 161.8%, and 200% for additional exits.

Pyramiding
- Add medium to smaller units to the existing position as the trade progresses.

- Add units at 50% or 61.8% Fibonacci retracement levels, aiming to do so on a retracement.

How does this strategy align with your trading objectives? Would you like to make any further adjustments?

I hope this comprehensive step through, of the development of a trading plan help you to better understand the process!

Chapter - From Theory to Practice

Trading Blueprint: From Novice to Pro Trader

Embarking on a trading journey can be a thrilling yet overwhelming experience. The "Trading Blueprint" provides a structured roadmap guiding beginners from their first foray into the world of trading to becoming adept, confident traders. It outlines key stages, significant milestones, and sets realistic expectations for each phase.

Stage 1: The Initiation

Objective: Familiarise with the basic terminologies and understand the foundational principles of trading.

- Milestone 1: Mastering Trading Lingo - From 'bids' to 'asks', 'bulls' to 'bears', get acquainted with the essential trading terms.

- Milestone 2: Setting up Your Trading Account - Selecting the right trading platform and understanding its functionalities.

- Expectation: At this stage, you might feel overwhelmed, but remember, every proficient trader started here. Stay persistent!

Stage 2: Dipping the Toes

Objective: Begin live trading with small amounts, focusing on learning rather than profiting.

- Milestone 1: First Live Trade - The unforgettable experience of executing your first trade, regardless of its outcome.

- Milestone 2: Understanding Market Behaviour - Recognizing basic patterns and how global events influence markets.

- Expectation: You might face losses, but treat them as learning opportunities. It's essential to maintain a trading journal for reflection.

Stage 3: Building Confidence

Objective: Enhance your trading strategies, improve decision-making, and begin diversifying your trades.

- Milestone 1: Consistent Trading Routine - Establishing a daily routine to assess markets, make trades, and review outcomes.

- Milestone 2: Expanding the Portfolio - Moving beyond your initial trading assets or pairs and exploring new markets.

- Expectation: This stage will see a mix of wins and losses. Embrace a growth mindset and continuously refine your strategies.

Stage 4: Advanced Trading Tactics

Objective: Delve into advanced trading techniques, tools, and analytics for informed decision-making.

- Milestone 1: Mastering Technical Analysis - Employing charts, indicators, and patterns to predict future market movements.

- Milestone 2: Fundamental Analysis Expertise - Understanding how economic news, company reports, and global events influence your trades.

- Expectation: While you'll become more adept, markets can be unpredictable. Stay humble, continue learning, and always prioritise risk management.

Stage 5: The Path to Proficiency

Objective: Achieve consistent profitability, expand your trading horizons, and potentially explore trading as a primary income source.

- Milestone 1: Crafting Your Unique Trading Strategy - Combining all learned techniques to create a personalised, effective trading method.

- Milestone 2: Continuous Learning and Adaptation - Markets evolve, and so should you. Stay updated with new tools, strategies, and market dynamics.

- Expectation: Achieving consistency in profitability and feeling confident in your trades. Remember, even at this stage, there's always more to learn.

This blueprint serves as a road map, ensuring you're well-equipped at every stage of your trading adventure. Whether you're celebrating a successful trade or learning from a misstep, remember to enjoy the process and grow with each experience.

Embracing the Concept of Continuous Improvement

Continuous improvement in trading is the practice of consistently analysing and refining your trading approach to enhance performance. It involves a commitment to learning from both successes and failures, and the willingness to adapt and evolve as markets change and new information becomes available. This ongoing process helps traders maintain a competitive edge and increase their proficiency over time.

Components of Continuous Improvement

Regular Review and Analysis: Conduct regular reviews of your trading activities, examining both winning and losing trades. Analyze the reasons behind the outcomes and identify patterns or recurring issues. This review should cover various aspects, including trade execution, risk management, and emotional responses.

Education and Learning: Continually seek to expand your knowledge base. This could involve studying market trends, economic indicators, new trading strategies, or psychological aspects of trading. The financial markets are dynamic, so staying informed about new developments and trading techniques is crucial.

Feedback Loops: Implement feedback loops into your trading process. This means using the information gained from your reviews and analysis to make informed adjustments to your trading plan. Feedback loops can help you correct mistakes, reinforce successful strategies, and adapt to changing market conditions.

Adapting to Market Changes: Markets evolve due to changes in economic conditions, market sentiment, and global events. Successful traders adapt their strategies to align with these changes. This might involve modifying technical indicators, adjusting risk management parameters, or exploring new asset classes.

Testing and Validation: Before implementing significant changes to your trading strategy, test them. This could be through backtesting using historical data, paper trading, or using a small portion of your capital to assess the effectiveness of the new approach. Testing helps minimise the risk of substantial losses and ensures that the changes are beneficial.

Setting and Reviewing Goals: Set clear, measurable goals for your trading activities and review them regularly. Goals should be realistic, achievable, and aligned with your overall trading strategy. Regular reviews allow you to assess your progress and make necessary adjustments to your goals and strategies.

Mindset and Psychological Resilience: Trading can be emotionally challenging. Developing a strong, resilient mindset is crucial for long-term success. This includes managing stress, maintaining discipline, and learning from mistakes without letting them negatively impact your confidence or decision-making.

Utilising Technology: Leverage technology to enhance your trading process. This can include using advanced charting tools, automated trading systems, or analytics platforms to gain deeper insights into market trends and improve trade management.

Implementing Continuous Improvement

Create a Structured Plan: Develop a structured plan for continuous improvement, outlining how and when you will review your trades, update your knowledge, and test new strategies.

Maintain a Trading Journal: Keep a detailed trading journal that records all your trades, market observations, and emotional states. This journal is a valuable resource for identifying what works and what doesn't.

Engage with a Community: Join trading forums, attend webinars, or participate in trading groups. Engaging with a community of traders can provide new insights, feedback, and support.

Seek Professional Feedback: Consider hiring a trading coach or seeking mentorship from experienced traders. Professional feedback can offer new perspectives and help identify areas for improvement that you might not have noticed.

Reflect and Reset: Regularly take time to reflect on your trading performance and overall approach. Use this time to reset your goals and strategies based on the insights gained through your continuous improvement efforts.

Conclusion

When trading, the mastery of trade management strategies stands as a cornerstone for achieving consistent success. I hope this exploration into the nuances of these strategies has given you a robust framework for navigating the markets. Lets recap on some of the important concepts.

Stop Loss Orders

A fundamental risk management tool, stop loss orders act as a safety net, automatically closing out a trade at a predetermined loss threshold. This mechanism is crucial for preserving capital by limiting potential losses on individual trades. The strategic placement of stop loss orders requires a careful analysis of market volatility and price patterns to avoid premature exits while still protecting against significant downturns.

Trailing Stops

As an evolution of the basic stop loss, trailing stops offer a dynamic approach to protect profits while allowing a trade to remain open to capture further upside. These orders adjust in response to favourable price movements, securing a portion of the accrued profits by "trailing" behind the market price at a set distance. This strategy harmonises the dual objectives of profit maximisation and loss minimization.

Profit Targets

Establishing profit targets is about setting specific goals for closing a trade when it reaches a certain level of profitability. This strategy helps traders to lock in profits at optimal points before market reversals can erode gains. Profit targets require a deep understanding of market behaviour and the ability to forecast potential price movements based on technical and fundamental analysis.

Position Sizing

The art of position sizing involves determining the appropriate volume of assets to trade based on the trader's risk tolerance and the overall account balance. This strategy ensures that the impact of any single trade is balanced against the trader's risk management objectives, preventing disproportionate losses and promoting long-term account growth.

Evaluating Trade Management Performance

A critical component of successful trading lies in the continuous evaluation of trade management performance. This evaluation requires a thorough analysis of trade outcomes, as well as the application of backtesting and forward testing to validate the effectiveness of trade management strategies. The aim is to refine these strategies over time, enhancing both risk management and the potential for favourable trade outcomes.

Analysis of Trade Outcomes

Regularly reviewing the outcomes of executed trades is essential for identifying patterns of success and areas for improvement. This analysis should cover various metrics, including the hit rate (percentage of profitable trades), average profit vs. average loss, and adherence to predefined risk management protocols. By understanding the strengths and weaknesses of their trade management approach, traders can make informed decisions on what adjustments may be necessary.

Backtesting

Backtesting involves applying trade management strategies to historical market data to assess how those strategies would have performed in the past. This process allows traders to simulate trading decisions without financial risk, providing insights into the viability and potential profitability of their strategies. Crucially, backtesting should account for transaction costs, slippage, and market liquidity to ensure realistic outcomes.

Forward Testing

Also known as paper trading, forward testing allows traders to apply their strategies in real-time market conditions without committing real capital. This form of testing is valuable for validating the practicality of a strategy under current market dynamics. It offers the benefit of experiencing the psychological aspects of trading—such as dealing with emotional responses to market movements—while maintaining a risk-free environment.

Iterative Adjustments

The evaluation process is inherently iterative, demanding ongoing adjustments to trade management strategies based on accumulated data and testing results. Adjustments might involve fine-tuning stop loss levels, modifying trailing stop parameters, or recalibrating position sizes in response to changing market volatility or personal risk tolerance levels. This iterative process is fundamental to evolving and improving a trade management system, ensuring it remains robust across different market conditions and trading phases.

The necessity for continuous evaluation underscores the dynamic nature of trading, where static strategies often fall short. By embracing an iterative approach to trade management evaluation, traders can enhance their risk management practices and improve the overall effectiveness of their trading outcomes. This ongoing process of evaluation and adjustment not only refines trade management strategies but also contributes to the personal growth and development of the trader, aligning their approach more closely with the realities of the financial markets.

The Role of Comprehensive Trade Management in Risk Management

Risk management is not merely a component of the strategy, it is the foundation upon which successful trading is built. A well-designed trade management system plays a pivotal role in effective risk management, acting as the guardian of a trader's capital and the facilitator of consistent trading performance. This part delves into how comprehensive trade management underpins risk management, limits losses, and bolsters trading consistency.

Foundation of Risk Management

At its core, a trade management system encompasses rules and strategies that dictate how trades are entered, managed, and exited. These rules are designed with the primary aim of minimising losses and protecting trading capital. Effective trade management involves not just the management of individual trades but also the oversight of overall market exposure and the alignment of trading activities with a trader's risk tolerance.

Limiting Losses

One of the key functions of trade management in risk management is the ability to limit losses. This is achieved through mechanisms such as stop loss orders, which ensure that a trade is exited at a predetermined level of loss, and trailing stops, which protect profits while allowing for the capture of additional gains. By defining the maximum acceptable loss per trade and adhering to it, traders can avoid the detrimental impact of large, unchecked losses on their trading capital.

Enhancing Trading Consistency

Consistency in trading is largely a function of managing variance in trade outcomes. A comprehensive trade management system helps in smoothing out the equity curve by mitigating the impact of losses and optimising the profitability of winning trades. Strategies such as scaling into and out of positions, using profit targets, and adjusting position sizes based on volatility are instrumental in achieving a consistent trading performance. These strategies ensure that traders are not disproportionately affected by any single trade outcome, promoting a steadier path towards long-term profitability.

Strategic Adaptability

A nuanced aspect of comprehensive trade management is its adaptability to changing market conditions. An effective trade management system includes criteria for adjusting trading strategies in response to market volatility, economic announcements, or shifts in market sentiment. This adaptability is crucial for risk management, as it allows traders to modulate their exposure in line with the prevailing risk environment, thereby avoiding potentially ruinous losses during periods of high uncertainty or adverse market movements.

Comprehensive trade management is the linchpin of effective risk management in trading. By systematically limiting losses, promoting consistency, and providing a framework for strategic adaptability, a well-crafted trade management system equips traders with the tools necessary to navigate the complexities of the financial markets. It underscores the importance of discipline, strategic foresight, and a commitment to continuous learning and adaptation in the pursuit of trading excellence.

Best Practices for Developing a Successful Trade Management System

Developing a successful trade management system is a multifaceted endeavour that requires careful consideration of one's trading strategy, risk tolerance, and objectives. The effectiveness of this system hinges on its alignment with the trader's personal approach and its flexibility to adapt to the ever-changing market dynamics. This section outlines the best practices for crafting a trade management system that can enhance trading performance and resilience.

Alignment with Personal Trading Strategy

The cornerstone of a robust trade management system is its alignment with the trader's overall trading strategy. Whether a trader prefers day trading, swing trading, or long-term investing, the trade management system must be tailored to complement these strategies. This involves setting appropriate trade entry and exit criteria, choosing suitable risk management tools, and determining the right timing for trade execution. A system that is in harmony with the trader's strategy enhances the likelihood of consistent trade execution and reduces the temptation to make impulsive decisions.

Adherence to Risk Tolerance and Objectives

Personal risk tolerance and trading objectives are critical factors in the design of a trade management system. Risk tolerance influences decisions on position sizing, leverage, and stop loss settings, ensuring that the trader remains comfortable with the level of risk undertaken in each trade. Trading objectives, whether they relate to income generation, capital growth, or portfolio diversification, should dictate the selection of markets, assets, and timeframes. By embedding personal risk tolerance and objectives into the trade management system, traders can pursue their goals with confidence and clarity.

Integration of Multiple Trade Management Strategies

To build a resilient trade management system, integrating multiple strategies is essential. This integration allows traders to navigate different market conditions and effectively manage trades under various scenarios. For instance, combining fixed and trailing stop loss orders can provide both downside protection and the flexibility to capture upside potential. Similarly, using a mix of technical and fundamental analysis can offer a more comprehensive view for making informed trade decisions. The inclusion of diverse strategies ensures that the trade management system remains robust and versatile, capable of adapting to market volatility and trends.

Adaptability to Changing Market Dynamics

The financial markets are inherently dynamic, with conditions that can change rapidly due to economic data releases, geopolitical events, or shifts in market sentiment. A successful trade management system must, therefore, be designed with adaptability in mind. This means regularly reviewing and adjusting the system based on market feedback and personal performance. Traders should be prepared to modify their strategies in response to new information or changes in market conditions to protect their capital and take advantage of emerging opportunities.

The development of a successful trade management system is a deliberate process that requires a deep understanding of one's trading style, risk tolerance, and goals. By aligning the system with these personal attributes and integrating a variety of strategies, traders can create a flexible and resilient framework. This framework not only guides them through the complexities of the markets but also enhances their ability to achieve sustained trading success.

Trading is not just about making decisions on when to enter and exit the market; it's about making those decisions with a clear understanding of risk, a strategic framework for managing that risk, and the flexibility to adapt as market conditions change. The strategies and principles discussed in this text serve as a compass, guiding traders through the tumultuous seas of financial markets toward the shores of success.

As we conclude this journey through trade management, it's important to recapitulate the core principles that form the foundation of effective trading. We started by understanding the essence of trade management and its pivotal role in crafting a successful trading strategy. We delved into the intricacies of aligning trade management with personal trading goals, ensuring that every decision is made with clear objectives in mind.

We explored adaptive trade management, highlighting the importance of adjusting strategies to meet the ever-changing market conditions. This adaptability is crucial for staying relevant and profitable in the market trading environment. We also underscored the significance of position sizing as a fundamental element of risk management, ensuring that each trade is proportionate to individual risk tolerance and overall trading capital.

Throughout our journey, we emphasised the necessity of continuous improvement—a commitment to learning, analysing, and refining your trading approach. This ongoing process helps in identifying strengths and weaknesses, learning from both successes and failures, and staying updated with the latest market trends and trading techniques.

Trade management is not just a set of rules to follow but a mindset to cultivate. It's about making informed decisions, managing risk, and adapting to new challenges. The principles and strategies outlined in this guide are meant to serve as a foundation upon which you can build and customise your own approach.

Embrace the continuous learning curve in trading with enthusiasm. Each trading day presents a new set of challenges and opportunities to learn and grow. Adapt to market changes with agility, viewing them not as obstacles but as stepping stones to greater understanding and proficiency. Let each trading experience, whether a win, a loss, or a draw, be a lesson in itself, contributing to your growth as a trader.

Remember that the path to trading mastery is not linear. It is filled with highs and lows, successes and setbacks.

May your trading journey be fruitful, your strategies sound, and your resolve unwavering. Here's to your continued success in the markets, armed with effective trade management strategies that stand the test of time and change.